The Fugitive Poets

Southern Classics Series

M. E. Bradford, Editor

D0167795

Southern Classics Series

M. E. Bradford, Series Editor

The Fugitive Poets

Modern Southern Poetry in Perspective

Edited by
WILLIAM PRATT

with a revised, updated
introduction by William Pratt

Cover painting by Paul Davis

J. S. Sanders & Company
NASHVILLE

Due to space constraints, acknowledgments
appear on page 169.

Library of Congress Catalog Card Number:
91-62453

ISBN: 1-879941-00-7

Published in the United States by
J. S. Sanders & Company
P. O. Box 50331
Nashville, Tennessee 37205

Distributed to the trade by
National Book Network
4720-A Boston Way
Lanham, Maryland 20706

1991 printing
Manufactured in the United States of America

To

THE FUGITIVES

wherever they have fled

Contents

Preface

The first issue of *The Fugitive* magazine appeared in Nashville, Tennessee, in 1922, and with it the major period of modern Southern literature began. It was a modest, but a timely, beginning, for a school of poets and critics that would afterwards lead the way in many of the important developments in poetry, fiction, and criticism, not only in the South, but elsewhere in the country. Their achievement is amply documented in articles, books of criticism, and volumes of literary history, but no comprehensive collection of Fugitive poetry was published between 1928, shortly after the magazine ceased publication, and 1965, when the first edition of this anthology appeared. The need for a second anthology was great, for the major works of most of the poets were written, or much revised, after the first anthology. Now there is need for a third anthology, revised and expanded to include more works by the original poets, along with additional poems by poets not included in the second anthology. Many readers understandably confuse the Fugitives with the Agrarians and the New Critics, two later schools they helped to found. But the Fugitives were first and foremost poets, and the aim of this revised anthology is to present a more generous and comprehensive selection of their poems, some early and some late, together with an expanded account of their history as a literary school, and their further accomplishments as individual poets.

By now, many Fugitive poems are classics, and many others deserve to be. To see the Fugitives in perspective is to view a body of poems impressive in number and scope, worthy of a great period of literature in the South and in the nation. It is also to take stock of a corporate achievement that rivals any in American literary history. This revised anthology offers further proof that the Fugitives, whatever their individual accomplishments, still belong together as one of the most durable and influential schools in modern American letters.

In Pursuit of the Fugitives

I have run further, matching your heat and speed,
And tracked the Wary Fugitive with you ...
JOHN CROWE RANSOM, "Ego"
(from the first issue of *The Fugitive*)

I. THE FUGITIVES AS A LITERARY SCHOOL

A. The Fugitives and the Imagists

Modern American poetry abounds in individualism, but two groups of poets have affected its course profoundly. The first of these called themselves "Imagists"; the second called themselves "Fugitives." The Imagists gathered in London, in the period from 1909–1917, and beginning in 1913, published their poems in *Poetry* magazine and *The Little Review* in Chicago, and in *The Egoist* in London. The Fugitives began gathering in Nashville, Tennessee, about 1915, and gained their fame from a magazine they named *The Fugitive*, which they edited and published during the years 1922–1925. The Imagists may have shown greater initiative in getting the modern movement under way, but the Fugitives showed greater perseverance in directing its course, until it has become an open question which of the two groups has played a more decisive role in the shaping of modern American poetic style. If we judge style as *technique*, meaning new ways of using words, then clearly the Imagists have dominated, for English poetic diction and rhythm were noticeably altered by their emphasis on verbal economy, imagery, and free verse; but if we judge style as *character*, meaning emphasis on theme, on moral and intellectual qualities embodied in words, on the human figure at the center of a poem, then it is the Fugitives who have played the decisive role, for no other group of American poets in the twentieth century has combined so much subtlety with so much certitude.

The two groups may best be seen as essential, but complementary, forces. The relation between them is in a sense a historical succession, with the Imagists flourishing first, in the decade surrounding the First World War, and the Fugitives coming afterward, in the decade of the Twenties. But in the long view, it is as if one movement was bound to have its counterpart in the other. The Imagists were above all internationalists, individualists, and experimentalists; the Fugitives were above all regionalists, traditionalists, and classicists. Between them, they embodied all the main influences at work in the American Literary Renaissance of the twentieth century, and included many of the major poets that came to prominence in the first half of the century. What can be seen most clearly, in comparing the Imagists with the Fugitives, is that the vigor of literary expression in the modern period has come from a creative opposition between what might be called the "Romantic" imagination and what might be called the "Classical" imagination. Neither imagination existed in its pure state: there was tension within them, for there was much in the Imagists that was Classical (the poems of H.D., and some of Pound's and Aldington's, read like translations from the Greek—and some of them are), and much in the Fugitives that was Romantic (the shade of Keats's "Ode to a Nightingale" lurks behind such an apparently classical poem as Ransom's "Philomela," and Warren's "Ballad of Billie Potts" is one of the finest long poems in free verse written in the entire modern period). But the Imagist stress on freedom needed the Fugitive stress on form as a counterbalance, and the attack on tradition implied in the Imagist experiments needed to be corrected by the respect for tradition implied in much Fugitive practice.

Perhaps the one person who could see this action and reaction at the time was John Gould Fletcher, the sole poet who participated in both groups. Being at once an expatriate and a Southerner, Fletcher became a leading member of the Imagists in their later phase when Amy Lowell was making them into "Amygists," and a few years afterward he joined the distinguished company of outside contributors to *The Fugitive*, which included Robert Graves and Hart Crane, among others. In 1927, shortly after *The Fugitive* magazine had ceased publication, Fletcher wrote a short essay on "The Two Elements in Poetry."[1] His position was that the "free verse" school of Imagists under Ezra Pound had run its course, and that a new "Classical" school had been formed in the Twenties, under the general leadership of T. S. Eliot, but best represented as a school by the Southern Fugitives. This new school was more sophisticated than the Imagists, he said, for:

> It takes the innovations of form of the free-verse school more or less for granted; what it quarrels with is fundamentally their attitude toward art. It begins by challenging the importance of emotion in poetry: it asserts that intellect and not emotion is the true basis of poetic art; and it proposes a return to classicism as the only possible remedy for the common looseness and facility of much present-day poetic art.

In his brief survey of the two schools, Fletcher went so far as to suggest that the difference between them was ultimately regional, for most of the Imagists were from the North and West, with Chicago as the center of publication, while the new Classicists were mostly from the East and South, with Nashville, Tennessee, as the publishing center. He did not say what the close relation between Eliot, the "Easterner" from St. Louis, and Pound, the "Westerner" from Philadelphia, meant to American poetry—this was an anomaly that could not be accounted for in terms of region—but he did maintain with good reason that "The main impulse in the early development of this school of intellectual poetry in America was the publication for a few years shortly after the war of the magazine called *The Fugitive*, by a small group centering about Nashville, Tennessee."

The Fugitives were by that time near the end of their close and productive association, which had begun informally as early as

[1] *Saturday Review of Literature*, IV (Aug. 27, 1927), 65–66.

1915, and which was to end formally with the publication in 1928 of their only collection of poems, entitled *Fugitives: An Anthology of Verse*, brought out in New York by Harcourt, Brace—indicating that their poetry had a national audience already. Although it was the last official Fugitive publication, it did not mark the end but the beginning of distinguished literary careers for several of the Fugitives. Like the Imagists, the Fugitives disbanded too early to produce a fully representative volume of their poetry, yet the value of their individual achievements can best be seen in the perspective of their achievement as a group. It may then be recognized that, while the Imagists were truly a literary "movement"—original, exciting, revolutionary in impulse, alive with the unexpressed possibilities of the present—the Fugitives have been truly a literary "school"—disciplined, deliberate, conscious of an immense indebtedness to the past. Somewhere between the poles of the Imagist "movement" and the Fugitive "school," much of the best American poetry of the twentieth century has been written.

B. A History of the Fugitive School

Louise Cowan begins her authoritative account, *The Fugitive Group: A Literary History*,[2] with this definition: "The Fugitives were a quite tangible body of sixteen poets who, having no particular program, met frequently from 1915 to 1928 for the purpose of reading and discussing their own work." Of the sixteen poets she names,[3] only six (Ransom, Tate, Warren, Davidson, Moore, Riding) have had anything like a national reputation, and of these six, only four (Ransom, Tate, Warren, Davidson) have achieved what might be called a lasting fame (though the reputation of Laura Riding, which has depended too long on her association with Robert Graves, may come to be recognized in its own right). Yet the significance of the group as a group was that it included a wide variety of individuals, some of

[2] Baton Rouge: Louisiana State University Press, 1959.

[3] They are: John Crowe Ransom, Allen Tate, Robert Penn Warren, Donald Davidson, Merrill Moore, Laura Riding, Walter Clyde Curry, Jesse Wills, Alec Brock Stevenson, Sidney Mttron Hirsch, Stanley Johnson, William Yandell Elliott, William Frierson, Ridley Wills, James Frank, and Alfred Starr.

whom would have been dedicated poets if they had never met, and some of whom were accidentally drawn into a literary circle whose eventual fame went far beyond any ambitions they had when they joined it. The formation of the group was entirely fortuitous, without any serious purpose beyond the pleasure of good fellowship and warm hospitality, and the stimulation of argument among intelligent people. Far from beginning as a self-conscious group of writers with a set of theories to put into action (as the Imagists, for example, began), the Fugitives were at first nothing more than a gathering of friends, some of whom were teachers, some students, and some simply businessmen, who enjoyed one another's company. That they became something more consequential was as much a historical accident as their coming together in the first place, for they were in the strict sense of the word *amateurs*, "lovers" of everything from good food (of which there was always an abundance at Fugitive meetings) to good manners, fascinating people (at the center of the group was a Jewish intellectual, artist's model, and world traveler named Sidney Hirsch, whose habit was to recline on a couch and deliver opinions magisterially), and above all good talk, which was never lacking, whatever the subject. In short, this was one group of poets whose writing came directly out of their interest in one another; they had no purpose to pursue beyond that of friendship, in the Greek sense of *philia*, the mutual attraction of like-minded people. What began as simply an informal fraternity, or philosophers' club, developed by gradual stages into a serious literary school with its own journal, and an audience that reached beyond the city into the region, the nation, and the world. As Mark Van Doren commented, when the first Fugitive anthology appeared in 1928:

> I am convinced that the way taken by the Fugitives toward poetry is one of the best ways—it was the way, incidentally, of the thirteenth-century Italian poets, of the symbolists in France, and of certain late nineteenth-century English and Irish poets. It is the way of friendship and discussion; it is the way of the amateur society . . .[4]

[4] Mark Van Doren, "First Glance," *Nation*, CXXVI (March 14, 1928), 295.

The history of the Fugitives is a history of how friendship flowered into art, and it is of particular interest in a country that has
always prided itself on the Horatio Alger story of singular, self-
reliant success. Co-operation, instead of competition, would
seem to be the secret behind Fugitive accomplishment.

1. THE FUGITIVES: INFORMAL PHASE, 1915–1921

In his later reminiscence about the Fugitive period, John Crowe
Ransom gave a concise account of how the group transformed
themselves from casual friends into serious poets:

> "We began to gather for conversation at the house of Sidney
> Hirsch. The conversations became more frequent and finally they
> became regular on the calendar, and after we talked ourselves out,
> we said: 'Well, the next thing to do is to get some of this written
> down.' And presently, it began to be written in verse, and pretty
> soon we were exchanging verses, and that seemed to be a very
> natural sequence."[5]

The only thing left out of Ransom's account of how the Fugitives evolved as a literary school is the amount of serious effort
and imagination that went into the formation of a poetic school
in the South, that "Sahara of the Bozart" as H. L. Mencken had
jokingly called it, where nothing of such eminence had existed
before. To see how it grew into self-consciousness and later into
articulation, one needs more than this casual statement by the
acknowledged leader of the group. One needs the statements by
other Fugitives, notably Allen Tate's witty memoir, "*The Fugitive
1922–1925: A Personal Recollection Twenty years After*,"[6] and
Donald Davidson's more sober recollection, "The Thankless
Muse and Her Fugitive Poets,"[7] as well as the complete history of
the group, enriched with letters exchanged during the Fugitive
period, which has been so carefully compiled by Louise Cowan.

[5] "Upon Returning: An Interview with John Crowe Ransom," *Vanderbilt
Alumnus*, Vol. 47 (March–April, 1962), 45.

[6] *The Princeton Library Chronicle*, III, 3 (April, 1942), 75–84.

[7] *Southern Writers in the Modern World* (Athens: University of Georgia Press,
1958), 1–30.

From these sources,[8] it is possible to see how a small group of dedicated men were able to break through the tired rhetoric of the genteel tradition—the only tradition that existed in Southern letters before 1920—and begin building up a powerful critical intelligence that was capable of expressing itself first in lyric and narrative poetry, and later in fiction, literary criticism, and social essays.

It all seems to have started in a very offhand way. In 1915, a group of young teachers and students at a small, quiet southern university became informally acquainted with one another, partly through the old-fashioned custom of paying court to young ladies at their homes, but chiefly through the attractive personality of a gifted and eccentric young man who liked to have an audience for his ideas, especially if the audience was learned. He had almost no formal education to his credit, but had traveled and read widely, and had written and produced what someone called "the most artistic and ambitious spectacle ever given in the South"—a Greek pageant named "The Fire Regained," with a cast large enough for a Hollywood epic, intended to bring recognition to Nashville as "The Athens of the South" and set in the new replica of the Parthenon which had been painstakingly built to scale in Nashville's Centennial Park (Davidson's satirical verse portrait "On a Replica of the Parthenon" would later offer a quite different response). He had a talent, apparently, for organizing artistic ventures, and a greater talent for impressive conversation, so that he was able to draw around him a group of unusually intelligent young men and inspire them to creative activity—much as Gertrude Stein did in Paris in the twenties. In fact, allowing for the differences between a provincial capital and an international capital, Gertrude Stein and Sidney Hirsch were much alike, both freewheeling egotists with a flair for the arts, who delighted in giving and receiving flattery, both adept at extracting homage from younger people more gifted and brilliant

---

[8] After the first edition of this anthology appeared, *The Fugitive* was reprinted in a single volume (*The Fugitive: April, 1922 to December, 1925*, Gloucester, Mass: Peter Smith, 1967) and Donald Davidson, in introducing it, certified that: "William Pratt's introduction to his anthology of Fugitive poetry (Dutton) is historically sound . . . ," iv.)

than themselves. The hospitality of Sidney Hirsch's home was always magnanimous, whether it was provided by his sisters, as at first, or by his brother-in-law, James Frank, as later on in his comfortable house on Whitland Avenue, some distance west of the Vanderbilt campus, which today sports a historical marker to show that it was once a Fugitive gathering place. At any rate, the young professors and students at Vanderbilt found Sidney Hirsch's hospitality and his conversation irresistible.

By the summer of 1915, the nucleus of the Fugitive group was coming regularly to his house: John Crowe Ransom, an instructor of English fresh from a Rhodes Scholarship at Oxford; Donald Davidson, who like Ransom had come from a small Tennessee town and had acquired a thorough training in classical languages, and was working on a degree in English literature at Vanderbilt; Stanley Johnson, who like Ransom was teaching English; William Y. Elliott, who was interested in political science and later became a Rhodes Scholar and professor of government at Harvard (his most famous student would be Henry Kissinger); Alec Brock Stevenson, the son of a Canadian professor of Hebrew and a student of French as well as of classics; and Walter Clyde Curry, a South Carolinian who would later distinguish himself as a Chaucer scholar. The discussions were at first very general, and the early meetings were more philosophical than literary, the conversations being described simply as "Olympian," by one of the members of the group.

Then America entered the First World War, and the group broke up for a time, to reform itself again late in 1919, as the original members drifted back from overseas duty to the Vanderbilt campus. Meanwhile, they had kept up with one another by correspondence, and one of the members had achieved some amount of literary fame with his first book of poems. Ransom's *Poems About God* had been published in 1919, while the author was on duty in France, and had received favorable notice from such discerning judges as Robert Frost (who recommended its publication), Louis Untermeyer, and Robert Graves. Ransom returned as something of a hero to his friends, and from that time on he was the real leader of the group, though Sidney Hirsch retained the place of honor as host. They began to take the writing of poetry seriously now, with Ransom and Curry "trading" sonnets, and extending their discussion of them to an evening at the Jim Franks', where Sidney Hirsch held forth on "the symbolic aspects of etymology," a sort of mystical word game he had invented, and members began passing poems around for criticism. The pattern was set from which real poetry could emerge. The virtue of Hirsch was that he could imbue ordinary words with the power of occult wisdom, insisting always that poetry was a sacred art, and that all languages were really one language; while the virtue of Ransom was that he could offer poems of his own for others to criticize, and could make exhaustive criticism of their work. This combination of learned speculation on the history of words, and careful reading of new poems, followed by discussion of the strength and weakness of each individual offering, was the program at all Fugitive meetings from that time on.

Then, in 1921, a new member was admitted, and the group mind was appreciably deepened. Allen Tate, of Kentucky birth and Virginia "connections," was invited while a senior at Vanderbilt to join the group, and though he was the only student member at the time, he quickly became the intellectual gadfly who stung them into action. Though by his own admission, he was "not very consciously a poet" when he joined them, he soon became one, and his knowledge of modern poetry in English outstripped all the others, so that before long he was leading all the senior members by the nose into the intricacies of modern poetic style. Their response was reluctant, but immediate. Ransom, who had once traded sonnets with Curry, now showed his new poems to Tate, and in a short while Ransom was astonishing Tate with a poem in the new style that was to make him famous— a complex metaphysical style strikingly different from the conventionality of his first book, and quite definitely his own. As Tate himself described the moment of recognition later on:

John Ransom always appeared at the Fugitive meetings with a poem (some of us didn't), and when his turn came he read it in a dry tone of understatement. I can only describe his manner in those days as irony which was both brisk and bland. Before we began to think of a magazine John had written a poem which foreshadowed the style for which he has become famous; it was

"Necrological," still one of his best poems; I marvelled at it because it seemed to me that overnight he had left behind him the style of his first book and, without confusion, had mastered a new style.[9]

Thus it was Tate, the youngest member, who contributed the most modern point of view, and who also provoked the most violent disagreements—notably with Ransom, who made the mistake of reviewing T. S. Eliot's *The Waste Land* unfavorably, forcing Tate to rise publicly to its defense. This controversy occurred in 1922, a brilliant year for American poetry, since not only did Eliot's poem appear simultaneously in *The Criterion* in London and in *The Dial* in New York, but the first issue of *The Fugitive* appeared in Nashville.

2. THE FUGITIVES: FORMAL PHASE, 1922–1928

Experiment, discussion, revision—this was the discipline the group had learned by a process of mutual instruction in the years between their coming together and their venturing into print. By it, and their own considerable talents, they had mastered the technique of poetry. But skill in wielding words would not have made a poetic school. There had to be a creative spark among them to start the fire of inspiration, and there had to be a "sense of the age," an intuitive grasp of what most needed to be expressed at this moment of history. The creative spark was provided by Sidney Hirsch, who as presiding genius suggested, in the spring of 1922, that it was time to start a magazine. It is probable that he also provided the title of *The Fugitive* (though some thought it was Alec Brock Stevenson), and if so, it was his most original contribution, provocative enough and enigmatic enough to arouse the interest of the group and the curiosity of prospective readers. How the group acquired its "sense of the age" is more difficult to explain, for it appears that they had simply written enough good poems in seven years to make publishing a logical next step to take.

However, to anyone acquainted with the history of modern

[9] Tate, "*The Fugitive* 1922–1925," *loc. cit.*, 77–78.

literature, it must seem more than mere accident that these few serious minds should have expressed themselves in the period from 1922 to 1925, no matter how far removed from the center of things they might be. For these were the Golden Years of the modern age, the *Anni Mirabiles* as R.P. Blackmur called them, when suddenly an "explosion of talent took place" in the Western world that has dwarfed everything since, "crystallizing between 1922 and 1925 in *Ulysses, The Waste Land, The Magic Mountain, The Tower, The Counterfeiters*, and a great deal more."[10] *The Fugitive* magazine formed part of the "great deal more" that writers produced at this time, and whether it came about as an aftermath of the war, as some literary historians might argue, or as a direct revelation from heaven, as the more traditional theory of poetic inspiration would have it, there is no way to be sure. But that it was a crucial moment in history for a literary magazine to be launched, whatever the name and wherever the place, cannot easily be denied. If *The Fugitive* never assumed the commanding position in world letters occupied by Eliot's *Criterion*, it nevertheless began in the same year, and this speaks well for the contributors' sense of history. Its ending in 1925 may also be a point in their favor, coming from some awareness that the Golden Age could not last long, however arbitrary the reasons for stopping may really have been. History is not made by poets, but poets have a way of responding to it that often seems miraculous, and so it was, in a small way, with the Fugitives.

But for the Fugitives, to be conscious of their age meant to be conscious of their isolation from it: the title of their magazine implied a separation from the rest of mankind that became a perpetual theme of their poetry:

> And if an alien, miserably at feud
> With those my generation, I have reason
> To think to salve the fester of my treason:
> A seven of friends exceeds much multitude.

[10] R. P. Blackmur, "*Anni Mirabiles* 1921–25: Reason in the Madness of Letters," *Four Lectures Presented Under the Auspices of the Gertrude Clarke Whittall Poetry and Literature Fund* (Washington: Library of Congress, 1956), p. 10.

So wrote Ransom in his first poem, and so he and the others continued to write, in almost every poem and essay they contributed to the nineteen numbers of *The Fugitive* in the next three and a half years. The common theme was the alienation of the artist from his society, in this case a particular society, the American South: "THE FUGITIVE flees from nothing faster than from the high-caste Brahmins of the Old South," the opening statement declared. Against it ran the counter-theme of brotherhood within the group, the "seven of friends," a theme not so often stated as implied. The bond of friendship that first drew them together, and the practice of poetry that strengthened it, were evident in every page of the magazine, and nowhere more than in the editorial policy, which chose poems by ballot, and refrained from giving first place to any single member, passing the editorship from one poet to another throughout the course of the magazine. As an editorial in the sixth issue declared:

> We have no differentiation of ranks or titles, and even cling to an old-fashioned, roundabout method of group action in doing the chores of publication, with the very idea of securing the blessings of liberty against the possible suspicion of a tyranny.

In a conspicuous effort at anonymity, the members decided to choose pseudonyms for the first two issues of *The Fugitive*, though their better judgment soon brought them to reveal their identities. At any rate, the old literary game of pen names added a fillip for the local public, as one of the later Fugitives has testified:

> I was not a member of *The Fugitive* group from the beginning. I was invited to join after the first and before the second issue. I heard a great deal of its beginning from Allen Tate, Donald Davidson and John Crowe Ransom as well as from almost everyone else, for an enormous amount of local excitement arose among the undergraduates at Vanderbilt with the intimation that the first issue of a new poetry magazine was soon to appear. The fact that the authors used nom-de-plumes added an almost unbearable suspense to the advent of the first number. A village could not have been thrown into more titillation over the birth of a child whose paternity was in doubt, than the Vanderbilt campus

witnessed when poems appeared in *The Fugitive* by Roger Prim, Robin Gallivant, L. Oafer, Feathertop, Dendric and others.[11]

But behind the studied air of secrecy, a high intellectual tone was set with the opening issue, and this was maintained to the end: poems such as "Ego," by Ransom, "An Intellectual's Funeral," by Johnson, and "To Intellectual Detachment," by Tate, revealed the austerity of the poets' intentions, while at the same time reflecting an uneasiness about the dangers of spiritual pride, as if the authors felt trapped in their own self-consciousness and were struggling to escape it. Though none of them expressed the feeling as strikingly as T. S. Eliot had in "The Love Song of J. Alfred Prufrock," or Ezra Pound in "Hugh Selwyn Mauberley," the sense of intellectual alienation was one they shared with the leading poets of the age.

In the second issue, the Fugitives declared themselves to be "neither radical nor reactionary, but quite catholic in their tastes," and at the end of this issue they brought forth their first really distinguished poem: Ransom's "Necrological." This poem showed how much Ransom had matured in the few years since his *Poems About God*, for it displayed a new mastery of diction, blending the formal word with the colloquial phrase in a way that was to become one of Ransom's trademarks, and it displayed a wit that was present in every line, flavoring the elegant mannerism of his speech with the saving grace of humor, and adding a subtle self-irony that seemed to mock the apparent morbidity of the poem. Clearly, an original voice was speaking here, and it was to speak again in subsequent issues of *The Fugitive*. Ransom was the one member of the group who had arrived at full maturity as a poet when the magazine began, and who filled its pages with some of his finest work: "Philomela," "Conrad at Twilight," "Bells for John Whiteside's Daughter," "Captain Carpenter," "Old Mansion," "Blue Girls," "Tom, Tom the Piper's Son,"[12]

[11] Merrill Moore, *The Fugitive: Clippings and Comment Collected by Merrill Moore* (Boston, 1939), 10–11.

[12] Later versions of "Blue Girls" and "Tom, Tom the Piper's Son," retitled "The Vanity of the Blue Girls," and "The Vanity of the Bright Young Men," appear here, exactly as submitted by Ransom himself for the first edition of this anthology.

"Piazza Piece," and many other poems bearing the unmistakable stamp of his style were printed in *The Fugitive*. It was no wonder that some readers thought all the poems in the first issue had been written by one man, whose real name was Ransom.

But if Ransom was the major poet of the Fugitive period, other poets were emerging to challenge him, and some already gave promise of stout competition. Davidson's and Tate's epigrammatic skills were shown in such epitaphs as "Lines for a Tomb" and "Non Omnis Moriar," though neither had as yet found his distinctive voice. Merrill Moore's inexhaustible capacity for sonnets was evident in every issue after the first, and if he lacked the polish of the others, the deftness of his touch and casualness of his manner were welcome antidotes to the solemn gravity of much Fugitive verse. Besides these skilled practitioners, two new poetic discoveries were made in the course of *Fugitive* publication. Among the first to win the prizes that began to be offered in 1923 were Robert Penn Warren and Laura Riding. Warren was then a sophomore at Vanderbilt, a red-haired, gangly youth from Kentucky, and he became the youngest member of the Fugitive group—younger even than Tate, who in discovering him recognized him as "the most gifted person I have ever known." Warren's talent was precocious, and he responded at once to the encouragement of the older poets, so that by 1925 he was able to offer *The Fugitive* such a classic poem as "To a Face in a Crowd." Laura Riding, neé Reichenthal, who changed her name, when she first began submitting poems to *The Fugitive*, to Laura Riding Gottschalk, was the wife of a history professor at the University of Louisville, and almost as important a discovery as Warren, since she had the distinction of becoming the only feminine member of the Fugitives. Her philosophical poems in free verse stood out both for their originality and their maturity, and added freshness and spontaneity to every issue in which they appeared. (Her inclusion in the present revised anthology will be welcomed by readers who missed her in the first edition. Her omission from the earlier edition was not the choice of the editor, but was her own conscious choice to renounce poetry as "a lying word," a position which seems to have softened in the intervening quarter of a century.)

The Fugitive was unique among little magazines of the time, in that it was devoted exclusively to poetry, and included no prose except for occasional short editorials and reviews. The poetry was of a consistently high quality, and was offered without comment, as proof of the poets' belief that poetry should speak for itself. On the few occasions when one of the contributors— usually Ransom, Davidson, or Tate—did offer his views in prose, these were on the subject announced early in 1924: "the present state of poetry." For example, a running argument was conducted on the question of poetic form, with Ransom generally defending the English tradition of meter and rhyme, at which he had become such a skillful practitioner, and Tate defending the new school of Symbolists, particularly as represented by Eliot and Hart Crane. Tate was willing to assert that "an individualistic intellectualism is the mood of our age," and to argue that the common spoken language was not a sufficient norm for the modern poet, who must recognize, he said, that "the poet's vocabulary is prodigious, it embraces the entire range of consciousness." Though Ransom was resistant to modernism, especially to free verse as a new form, he had to admit that the Imagists had abolished "stilted platitudes" and "sentimental clichés," and his own poetry gave evidence of the Symbolist influence on poetic diction that Tate so vigorously defended. And it was in a late issue of the magazine that Ransom made his first definition of one of the key terms of modern poetic style, irony, calling it "the rarest of the states of mind, because it is the most inclusive; the whole mind has been active in arriving at it, both creation and criticism, both poetry and science." Thus the tenor of critical argument in *The Fugitive* was not preponderantly for either traditionalism or modernism, but rather formed a dialectic that concluded, in the final issue, with a strong argument by Davidson for the new experiments in poetic technique by T. S. Eliot, E. E. Cummings, and Wallace Stevens: "The strangest thing in contemporary poetry," he observed, "is that innovation and conservatism exist side by side."

Both the dialectic and the poetry ended officially in December, 1925, with a brief announcement in the final issue of *The Fugitive* that the magazine was being "suspended." The reason given was not lack of either the financial or the creative resources to continue, but a simple lack of time. The contributors had become so busy with their own work that they were unable to carry on the onerous job of editing a magazine, even though "No Fugitive dreamed in the beginning that our magazine would meet with the success that it has." All that could be promised for the future was that "The Fugitives will continue to hold their frequent meetings for the discussion of poetry and philosophy," for as they said with characteristic independence, "we were holding these meetings for years before the thought of publication was entertained, and we shall go on holding them after publication, for the time being, has stopped."

So ended one of the most successful little magazines in America, which had acquired fame in spite of the provinciality of its origin, and which had certainly improved the taste of the age for good poetry. As Ransom said later, looking back:

> That was a group effort beyond anything I have ever taken part in. Its quality was rare and fine as a piece of cooperation; I do not mean to be passing a judgment on the poetic output. That was no better than it should be, though I suppose it was good enough not to leave us looking foolish after so much pains. They were the best days I have ever had.[13]

II. THE FUGITIVES AT LARGE

By the time *Fugitives: An Anthology of Verse* was published in 1928, the group of poets that had once been so closely associated had broken up, and some of the most active members had gone elsewhere—Tate to New York, where he was involved with a much larger and more heterogeneous group of writers that included Hart Crane and E.E. Cummings, and Warren to California and then to Oxford as a Rhodes Scholar. The Fugitives were no longer together, but the sense of the compact between them remained alive and continued to affect them. This sense was perhaps best defined in a letter from Tate to Davidson in 1924, when the magazine was still being published and the group was gathering regularly at the Frank home on Whitland Avenue in

[13] Postcript to *The Fugitive: Clippings and Comment Collected by Merrill Moore*, 11.

Nashville, to read and criticize one another's poems. Tate wrote, in response to a new book of poems by Davidson:

> It is the occasion for a renewed consciousness of the meaning of our compact, that covenant which was more signifi-cant than either of us could guess on the day of its almost casual making. For my part, its significance is quite separate from any idea of the greatness or immortality [we may achieve].
>
> As you say, it is the life of adventure, and I say that the reason of this is that it is the life of the soul; and it is the life of the soul despite the incidental frustrations we meet and the merely human foibles we display and the temporary misunderstandings of the flesh that we may suffer . . .[14]

The Fugitives were first of all a group of friends, for whom poetry served as a means of human intercourse, a kind of verbal sacrament shared with one another, that for a few years was capable of constant renewal. Once the magic had worked, the members were free to go their own way. Some became successful business men, some became editors and critics, a few became national and international men of letters, and some simply went on being teachers, carrying the truths discovered in the pursuit of poetry into the teaching of literature, enabling them in time to bring about something like a revolution in the study of their subject. For, once they learned how to interpret poems from the inside, they were able to interpret every other experience in terms of the primary experience of poetic truth, and by this means render special service to modern letters, in relation to the univer-sity, to the South, and finally to the world.

A. The Fugitives and the University

The close relation between the Fugitives and a particular uni-versity in the South might lead one to believe that they set them-selves up from the start as "university poets," with official sponsorship and a ready audience. Such was hardly the case. The

---

[14] Letter quoted in part by Louise Cowan in *The Fugitive Group*, 163, and quoted in full in *The Literary Correspondence of Donald Davidson and Allen Tate*, edited by John Tyree Fain and Thomas Daniel Young (Athens: University of Georgia Press, 1974), 96–97.

university had brought them together, but it took little interest in them or their magazine until after they had won their fame. The only official action taken toward them was by the head of the English Department, Edwin Mims, "a Southern liberal of the old school," as Tate described him, who invited them all to lunch and urged them not to publish a magazine. They went ahead with it, anyway, knowing they were on their own, and proud enough of their independence to announce in one issue, "Of course *The Fugitive* has no sort of connection with any institution whatever." They won their way to official recognition by receiving the recognition of other poets, just as any poet or group of poets has had to do in the twentieth century, when "art for the artists' sake" has seemed to be the unwritten rule.

Once having gained their fame, however, they could hardly avoid sharing it with Vanderbilt, for the connection between them and the university remained close and friendly. Happily for them, they stayed "outside the walls," as far as any formal sanction was concerned, but they had a vast effect on the intellectual life within the walls. The literary tradition of Vanderbilt began with the Fugitives, and what remains of it still thrives on their reputation. Being as involved as they were with all aspects of campus life—as teachers, students, and alumni—their example continued to stimulate the academic mind long after the group had dissolved, with Ransom teaching there for another decade before going to Kenyon, and Davidson holding a major professorship until his retirement in 1964.

By common inclination, amounting to principle, the Fugitives retained their "amateur" status, yet became the most respected group of university poets in America. Not one of them earned a Ph.D., though as teachers, critics, editors, and poets they added luster to the names of numerous American academies, as far-flung as California, Louisiana State, Yale, Sewanee, Princeton, Minnesota, and Kenyon. Having been a poet first, each enjoyed a reincarnation as editor, Warren founding *The Southern Review*, Ransom *The Kenyon Review*, and Tate giving new distinction to *The Sewanee Review* during his brief editorship. It is not too much to say that the Fugitives helped to make the university a fit place for poets, a valuable pioneering role in a time when the university became the principal patron of the arts. Though many

American poets have attended universities and taught in them, the Fugitives remain the one outstanding poetic school which developed naturally from a campus environment. The fact that a university was as much the "native" environment for the Fugitives as the South tends to demonstrate that for a long time it was the last stronghold of European aristocratic culture in the midst of a thriving democratic society. If the American university is no longer such an aristocratic stronghold, being forced, like the South, to yield to egalitarian pressures, nevertheless, during the period when the Fugitives were most active, it could be said that the university *was* the South, or at least the most enduring part of it.

B. The Fugitives and the South

Something like this has to be said, in order to make clear the ambivalent role the Fugitives played as Southerners. That they were Southerners, there can be no doubt, as much as Robert Frost was a New Englander or Robinson Jeffers a Westerner. But from the first, their loyalties were mixed: "THE FUGITIVE flees from nothing faster than from the high-caste Brahmins of the Old South," they proclaimed in their first issue, and in all subsequent issues they continued to argue the point. There was at first no consciously regional bias in their poetry; in fact they quarreled publicly with what they took to be the restrictive view of Southern culture, as expressed in an editorial in *Poetry* magazine that seemed to call for a Southern poetry that would be nostalgically and quaintly local. When Harriet Monroe, the editor, disclaimed such a view in her next issue, *The Fugitive* editors explained that "we fear to have too much stress laid on a tradition that may be called a tradition only when looked at through the haze of a generous imagination." They made it clear that they were against both "atavism" and "sentimentality" in Southern writing, vices that were all too familiar in the "moonlight and magnolia" school that had arisen in the South after the Civil War. In an editorial in the June, 1924, issue of *The Fugitive*, Davidson listed among the "Fallacies of Modern Poetry" the assumption that "A Good Poet must have Local Color." He went on to explain:

Frost has written of New England, Sandburg of Chicago, but whatever is good in their poetry is good not merely because they wrote of specific places. Place is incidental; it is subordinate; it may even form a definite limitation, and perhaps does in the case of much American poetry. At the best, it is merely a picturesque addition, not the inner substance of poetry.

Perhaps the best evidence that the Fugitives were not sentimentally, but critically, Southern is to be found in their poetry, where the ironic tone cuts through the veil of myth surrounding the scenes and characters, and reveals the age and decay crumbling the Old South into ruin. Ransom wrote of the "*Antique* Harvesters" that peopled the Southern landscape, looking like figures from a tapestry rather than real farmers with a field to plow, and he made of his "Captain Carpenter" a figure of gentle mockery, a sort of Southern Don Quixote who courageously but weakly defended his code of honor, until finally there was nothing left of him but a carrion for the kites; and he pictured himself in "Old Mansion" as an "intruder" who looked hard at the "house whose legend could in no wise be brief," and mused:

> It was a Southern manor. One need hardly imagine
> Towers, white monoliths, or even ivied walls;
> But sufficient state if its peacock *was* a pigeon;
> Where no courts held, but grave rites and funerals.

The images of age and death that are present in so much Fugitive poetry are in one sense a link with the earlier Gothic South of Edgar Allan Poe ("Our Cousin, Mr. Poe" as Tate acknowledged in a discreetly appreciative essay), but they are also evidence of the obsolescence of Southern culture, and proof that the poets were much aware of its transience and fragility. In the most famous of Fugitive poems, Tate's "Ode to the Confederate Dead," there is a similar point of reference to earlier Southern poetry (specifically, Henry Timrod's brief "Ode" for the dedication of the Charleston cemetery, just after the Civil War) but an equally strong disclaimer of blind loyalty to the past:

> What shall we say who have knowledge
> Carried to the heart? Shall we take the act
> To the grave? Shall we, more hopeful, set up the grave
> In the house? The ravenous grave?

Though no solution is found to the poet's dilemma, poised as he is between an unrecoverable, heroic past and an indeterminate, chaotic present, he has no hope of clinging to remembered glories: the isolation of the figure in the cemetery is final, and his only consolation is that it is a common evil all men must face:

> Leave now
> The shut gate and the decomposing wall:
> The gentle serpent, green in the mulberry bush,
> Riots with his tongue through the hush—
> Sentinel of the grave who counts us all!

Tate's Southern version of *The Waste Land* shows man trapped in time, honoring the past but unable to live by it, a victim of his own self-consciousness, tempted like Narcissus to embrace his own image and drown, but too stoic to give in to the despair he feels in the presence of evil and death. As Davidson perceptively wrote to Tate after seeing an early manuscript version of the "Ode" in 1927: "Your *Elegy* is not for the Confederate dead, but for your own dead emotion . . ."[15]

There is much in Fugitive poetry, in fact, that directly parallels the experience so powerfully expressed in that other great writer of the modern South, William Faulkner, who was equally severe in criticizing the land he never ceased to love. To place Tate's "Ode" beside such novels as *Sartoris* or *The Sound and the Fury*, written at almost the same historical moment, is to see how strikingly they portray a common experience: that of the South in crisis, too weak to throw off the old shell of the past, so entangled in an outworn tradition that the only choice left to the sensitive individual is suicide, a choice actually taken by Bayard Sartoris and Quentin Compson in Faulkner's novels, and vividly imagined by the spokesman in Tate's poem. Only the tragic grandeur and sympathy of the portrayal in each case relieves the hopelessness of the human situation.

To place Faulkner beside the Fugitives is only to recognize the dominant roles they have played in the Renaissance of modern Southern literature. Between them, the spoils may be almost

[15] *The Literary Correspondence of Donald Davidson and Allen Tate, op. cit.,* 186.

equally divided. If Faulkner is unquestionably greater as an isolated genius, the Fugitives have been greater as a civilizing instrument in Southern letters. There is still no novelist the equal of Faulkner anywhere in the South, and there are still no poets who can compare with the Fugitives in sustained achievement. If Faulkner is the prize example of the natural talent, or what might be called the rewards of self-education, the Fugitives are the prize examples of the tutored talent, or the rewards of formal education. What bound them together as artists and men was loyalty to their native region, in spite of its decadence, and adherence to the old ideal of Jeffersonian Agrarianism.

This is not to identify the Fugitives with the Agrarians, which would only lead to confusion. The Fugitives and the Agrarians were two separate schools, one of which was exclusively literary, the other just as exclusively social and political. The Agrarians were not organized until after the Fugitives had disbanded, and then they included only four members—albeit the major ones— of the previous group: Ransom, Davidson, Tate, and Warren. The Southern Agrarians, whose symposium, *I'll Take My Stand*, aroused so much criticism as a "reactionary" social document, must be understood in the context of the Depression years, when radical solutions to the American financial crisis were being proposed on all sides. The Agrarians were political idealists of the South, who tried to take a broad view of the common predicament, and who believed as Jefferson had believed (and as Faulkner also believed) that human culture has its grass roots in agriculture: destroy the intimate relation between man and nature, their argument ran, and you destroy the fertility of human imagination, and with it both men's satisfaction with life and their pleasure in art. The belief in an agrarian society was too deeply rooted in Southern life and character to be easily outgrown, and when the crisis of the American industrial system came, it was natural for Southerners to turn to what they thought was the one sure way of sustaining life and character. The Fugitives had not been conscious regionalists; in fact, they had opposed the regional approach to poetry; but in becoming responsible critics of society, they discovered their regional bias. As Tate put it for the whole Fugitive group:

They were willing to draw upon all the resources of poetry that they knew, for it was obvious that their sectionalism, if it existed, and their nationalism, if that existed, would take care of themselves . . . Fugitive poetry turned out to be profoundly sectional in that it was supported by the prejudices, feelings, values, into which the poets were born.[16]

What is most Southern in Fugitive poetry is more than Agrarianism; it is a special compound of local qualities, some of which are historical, some geographical, and some temperamental. Among the historical, one would include the many Classical references, the Greek names and Latin phrases, that so richly season this poetry. The Fugitive poets, like the little girls in Katherine Anne Porter's story, *Old Mortality*, seem to have been brought up in the belief that "one should always have Latin, or at least a good classical poetry quotation, to depend upon in great or desperate moments." But the historical would also include the broad perspective from which these poets view the contemporary world:

> Where we went in the boat was a long bay
> A slingshot wide, walled in by towering stone—
> Peaked margin of antiquity's delay,
> And we went there out of time's monotone:

So begins Tate's "The Mediterranean," with a majestic sweep of space and time that seems to place one above the earth, looking down from a great height. Again,

> We are the children of an ancient band
> Broken between the mountains and the sea,

writes Warren, seeing his westward-moving race in a more tragic Exodus to the Promised Land, which they can never quite reach or claim. Southern poetry, like Southern culture, is heavy with the historical sense, which as T. S. Eliot defined it in a famous passage

compels a man to write not merely with his own generation in his bones, but with a feeling that the whole of the literature of Europe

---

[16] "American Poetry since 1920," *Bookman*, LXVIII (Jan., 1929), 504.

from Homer and within it the whole of the literature of his own country has a simultaneous existence and composes a simultaneous order.[17]

The geographical element is equally prominent in this poetry, not as quaint "local color," or painted backdrop, but as a felt relation to the land:

> Autumn days in our section
> Are the most used-up thing on earth
> (or in the waters under the earth)
> Having no more color nor predilection
> Than cornstalks too wet for the fire,
> A ribbon rotting on the byre,
> A man's face weathered as straw
> By the summer's flare and winter's flaw.

It must have been just such a stanza that inspired so cosmopolitan an American poet as Wallace Stevens to exclaim: "Mr. Ransom's poems are composed of Tennessee."[18] Reading through a collection of Fugitive poetry, one realizes anew that the South has a religion of place, a mystique of locale, that is impossible to define by any means except poetry. Southerners specialize in local deities, and can raise a wild bear into an image of God, as in Faulkner's *The Bear*, or can penetrate deep into the wilderness, as in Davidson's "Sanctuary," where

> Men have found
> Images carved in bird-shapes there and faces
> Moulded into the great kind look of gods.

This same Southern love of place is what forms half its temperament, for the slowness of motion and speech, the indolence and "drawl," as well as the hot-bloodedness, are properties the climate instills in all races of the South. The other half of the Southern temperament, however, is not a matter of climate, but

[17] "Tradition and the Individual Talent," *Selected Essays* (New York: Harcourt, Brace, 1950), p. 4.
[18] "John Crowe Ransom, Tennessean," Homage to John Crowe Ransom, *Sewanee Review*, LVI (Aug.–Sept., 1948), 368.

has to do with the feudal character of Southern society; it comes out in the courtly politeness of manner, the reverence for the aged and the dead, the sense of stability and permanence in human values—all vestiges of an older order of things. It does not matter that the South failed to establish this "old order" in the New World for more than a few generations, at most; what matters is that the feeling for a hierarchical social order remains, like the love of land and the faith in God, as a kind of essential rightness, to betray which would be to betray oneself, and to lose heart completely:

> True, it is said of our Lady, she ageth,
> But see, if you peep shrewdly, she hath not stooped;
> Take no thought of her servitors that have drooped,
> For we are nothing; and if one talk of death—
> Why, the ribs of the earth subsist frail as a breath
> If but God wearieth.

C. The Fugitives and the World

1. THE MEANING OF "FUGITIVE"

Though the poets dropped their pseudonyms, after two issues of *The Fugitive*, and revealed their proper names, they left the name of their magazine undefined. "It seemed to be a secret among us, though no one knew what the secret was," Ransom said many years later.[19] That it was a secret, even to members of the group, points to the esoteric nature of their compact, and links them with the Imagists before them, and still earlier, with the French Symbolists, the original group from which all modern poetry has sprung. But it points even further, to the necessary mystery surrounding poetry in all places and times, indicating its ultimately religious source. Sidney Hirsch may have been wrong in many of his fanciful etymologies, but he was right in his primary intuition that poetry is a sacred art, an attempt always to translate the Word of God into the words of men, and he is

[19] *Fugitives' Reunion*, ed. R. R. Purdy (Nashville: Vanderbilt University Press, 1959), 122.

usually credited with inventing the name "Fugitive." What he may have meant by it remains a mystery, but was probably best explained by Tate, who put it that "A Fugitive was quite simply a Poet: the Wanderer, or even the Wandering Jew, the Outcast, the man who carries the secret wisdom of the world."[20] The shared belief of the Fugitives that poetry was something more than a pastime or diversion, that it was truly a divine calling, gave a dimension to their work that made even the most trivial poem seem somehow to participate in the universal human experience, passing beyond the limitations of the provincial.

Besides the esoteric sense of the term "Fugitive," there was also what might be called the emergent sense: that defined by the poems themselves. It is this sense that now gives fullest meaning to the word, in the light of more than half a century of accumulated poetry. In its emergent sense, the term "Fugitive" becomes one of the prime equivalents for "modern man." For, contrary to their desire to recover an older, communal experience of men living together on the land they loved—call it the "Old South," the "Golden Age," the "Garden of Eden," what you will—the pull of modern experience forced them to express recurrent images of isolation and alienation. The Fugitives, like other modern artists, had their Existential moments of despair, and were brought to face loneliness as a permanent human condition. It is to be found in the earliest of their poems, as in the lines of Warren's "To a Face in a Crowd":

> we must meet
> As weary nomads in this desert at last,
> Borne in the lost procession of these feet.

It appears again in Davidson's "Sanctuary," and even more eloquently, in his late, fine tribute, "Lines Written for Allen Tate on his Sixtieth Anniversary," which speaks of

> us, deliberate exiles, whose dry rod
> Blossoms athwart the Long Street's servile rage
> And tells what pilgrimage greens the Tennessee sod.

[20] *"The Fugitive 1922–1925," loc. cit.,* 79.

The "weary nomads" and the "deliberate exiles" are other names for the Fugitives, who could not flee from the common fate of man in this century. Most convincing of all is Warren's "Ballad of Billie Potts," a story of outlaws in western Kentucky told to him as a child, which has essentially the same plot as Albert Camus' *Le Malentendu* (*The Misunderstood*), the strange Existential drama of a murder occurring in eastern Europe. It is unlikely that Warren's poem and Camus' play have a common source, but there is no mistaking the similarity of character and theme, for both are parables of the Prodigal Son in reverse: they show that when human identity becomes lost, man becomes a prey to man, and even parents may be brought by unforeseen circumstances to murder their own child.

To stress the Existential meaning of the name "Fugitive" is only to suggest that the poetry of the modern South, like the fiction of the modern South, has been as much an expression of the age we live in as the literature of any other region. What gives Southern writing its special perspective is the sense of the distance, in time and space, between the South as a last remnant of European feudal society, with a landed gentry and a peasantry still rooted to a single spot of earth, and the largely undifferentiated mass society of the modern industrialized metropolis, with its restless and haunted multitudes. Fleeing from a vanishing culture into a relatively cultureless world, the Southern writer has experienced a profounder sense of shock than many of his contemporaries—except for those expatriate Americans like Eliot and Pound, who made the long voyage from the New World to the Old, and who lived in a different kind of exile during their distinguished and controversial careers.

2. THE FUGITIVES AS INDIVIDUALS

Yet it would not be fair to stress too much the common theme of their poetry, and ignore the achievements that each has made as an individual poet. For the group fostered individuality, in spite of its unity, and each main member was a distinguished practitioner of the art of poetry through a long lifetime.

Ransom's famous irony, for him the most inclusive of poetic

attitudes, was expressed with great subtlety and refinement in a body of poetry that is among the chief ornaments of the age. Being the oldest member of the group, Ransom came nearest in his poetry to expressing the traditional values of an earlier society, so much so that certain of his poems seem almost of another age, an age more dignified, polite, and gracious than ours, which always commands his admiration and obeisance. He achieved the classic simplicity of "Bells for John Whiteside's Daughter" and "Janet Waking," perhaps the finest poems about children written in the modern era. Yet even in these portraits of innocence, there is the jarring word that shakes the reader's confidence: we are "vexed" at the "brown study" of John Whiteside's daughter, and it is a "transmogrifying bee" that kills Janet's pet hen. The detachment of the poet is felt as keenly as his sympathy, just at the crucial moment when the feeling is deepest, and we are left wondering what he really thinks. A doubleness of vision pervades Ransom's poetry, until one begins to believe that "The Equilibrists" is his most characteristic poem of all—that memorable elegy for the lovers who can never decide between Heaven and Hell, honor or pleasure, and who die still undecided, in "their torture of equilibrium." Poetically, Ransom sometimes seems to be enjoying his eloquence while he is mocking it, as if he were Henry James on a holiday. Ransom's humor is at its broadest in such an early poem as "Amphibious Crocodile," a delicious caricature of the American abroad that languished in the back pages of *The Fugitive* until it appeared in the first edition of this anthology, but it is to be seen as well, peeking through the lines of the better-known, more plaintive "Philomela," one of the few "university poems" any of the Fugitives ever wrote:

I pernoctated with the Oxford students once,

Ransom says, remembering, from his own student days in England, that "pernoctated" was Oxford slang for staying out all night, but the tongue that utters it is in the cheek; self-irony is always present when Ransom speaks, so that even when his manners are most elegant, he is still slyly smiling. Ransom is the true Classicist, always polishing and perfecting his poems by a slow process of revision until they attain inevitability (for proof, compare the earlier version of "Tom, Tom the Piper's Son," which appeared in *The Fugitive*, with "The Vanity of the Bright Young Men" printed in this volume[21]). Yet he confided to me once that what is arguably his most perfect poem, "Bells for John Whiteside's Daughter," was written in a couple of days, and not a word of it was ever changed after its first publication in *The Fugitive*. Steeled by Ransom's gentle irony, the South may be seen almost accommodating itself to the harsh realities of "an unseemlier world," though not without a wistful backward look at the lost felicities of the "Old Mansion."

Not so with Davidson, who seemed able to bear the loneliness of exile better than the loneliness of the crowd. His "Lee in the Mountains" pictures the greatest Southern hero, Robert E. Lee, as accepting defeat with calm dignity, retiring from the battles of the Civil War to a place of contemplation, a university seat in the mountains of Virginia, as President of what was to become Washington and Lee University, and, remembering the "lost forsaken valor," waiting for death to come and claim him. Davidson, who of all the Fugitives remained nearest the place of their conclave, also remained the most convinced Southerner, the least ironic in his loyalty to the "Sanctuary" of the Southern wilderness and the "Hermitage" built by his forefathers. Yet there is an earnestness in his tone, there is a stubborn strength in the hard contours of his poetry that cannot easily be dismissed, and he has a gift for narrative verse that is rare in the modern age, shared only among the Fugitives by Warren. Davidson's ballad-like style is the result of long schooling in the oral tradition of the Southern mountains, a tradition which he often praised in his prose essays. He accepted his isolation stoically, like a man long accustomed to solitude, used to the silence of the mountains and the woods. He was once, however, the main cementing force of the Fugitives, and paid the group its most memorable poetic tribute in "Lines Written for Allen Tate on His Sixtieth Anniversary," which recalls the fervor of conversation in the old days when "that household's/Oaken being spoke like a plucked lyre." Of all the Fugitives, Davidson stayed closest to the oral tradition of the ballad and folktale, which unites

[21] For analysis and comparison of *fourteen* different versions of this poem, some of which were sent to me by Ransom as I was editing the first edition of this anthology, see "Metamorphosis of a Poem," in the Special John Crowe Ransom Issue of *Mississippi Quarterly*, XXX (Winter 1976–77). 29–58.

His children and His children's children forever
Unto all generations of the faithful heart.

Tate, on the other hand, is the convinced cosmopolitan, the "Easterner" among Southerners, who was most strongly drawn toward Eliot and Pound, and who competed with them in the complex sophistication of his verse. His "Ode to the Confederate Dead" stands at the center of modern Southern poetry, yet its theme—as he himself explained it in the classic essay of self-analysis, "Narcissus as Narcissus"—is not Southern but universal; it speaks of the dangers of solipsism, of a destructive self-love that is the sole modern substitute for the redemptive love of God. Tate was a generation younger than Ransom and Davidson in his attitude toward the world, the avowed modernist within the group, who fought hard for a new poetic style, and in his poetry did not shrink from obscurity or profundity, being possessed of a keen intelligence that leaped from image to image and insight to insight without recourse to logical transition. Both obscurity and profundity were ingrained in Tate's poetic style from the first, and it was only natural that he should move toward religious mysticism in his later poetry, culminating in "The Seasons of the Soul," which compares as a Christian meditation with Eliot's *Ash Wednesday* and *Four Quartets*. Tate's Southern Symbolism places him nearer the mainstream of modern poetry than any of the Fugitives, and though the long autobiographical poem that began with "The Swimmers" was never completed (he said only that he "hoped" to finish it some day), it is one of the finest examples of sustained *terza rima* in English poetry, not simply an imitation but a re-creation of the verse form of Dante's *Divine Comedy*, which has been the despair of so many gifted poets in languages other than Italian. Tate's seriousness, even when it is at its most obscure, is never a pretense, but an actual wrestling with the angel. His poetic style at its best stands somewhere between what he called the "angelic" imagination (that of Poe or Shelley, which leaps directly upward toward the infinite), and the "symbolic" imagination (that of Dante or Eliot, which moves from earth to heaven by perceptible stages of finite experience). Tate is the most difficult of the Fugitives, and probably also the most central, for in his poetry the traditional and the modern, the

Romantic and the Classical are inextricably intertwined, in a rich chiaroscuro of meanings, a tone at once "gallant and grave."

Then comes "The Kentucky voice of Warren," which is, in comparison with Tate's, the most "Western" of Southern voices. Warren was the one Fugitive whose experience incorporated the frontier, as well as the town, the plantation, and the farm, and his verse possesses a kind of rustic vitality that the other Fugitives (except Davidson) lack. He competes with Robinson Jeffers in his mastery of the long, controlled line, best suited for narrative, and he writes with a prose realism very near the naturalistic American fiction he knew so well. It is significant that one of his poems is titled "Original Sin: A Short Story," and his "Ballad of Billie Potts" is the nearest thing to a novel in free verse; at his best, he combines the swift pace of fiction with the intensity of poetry. As Tate predicted soon after meeting Warren as a student at Vanderbilt: "That boy's a wonder—has more sheer genius than any of us; watch him: his work from now on will have what none of us can achieve—power."[22] The power of Warren's poetry is often ominous: his finest early collection, *Eleven Poems on the Same Theme*, shows a preoccupation with the guilt of man, with the "Crime" that all men try to conceal from themselves, and with the predestined "Pursuit" of man by the omnipresent, relentless furies of his own conscience. Warren, the youngest of the group, was in many ways the most Fugitive of them all, and in this sense also the most modern. Yet there was always in Warren's poetry a strong countertheme, expressed unforgettably in his classic early poem, "Bearded Oaks":

> We live in time so little time
> And we learn all so painfully
> That we can spare this hour's term
> To practice for eternity.

Through the vivid contrast between the flight of man down the long corridors of time, and the eternal, timeless peace of the great moss-hung oaks, joy is brought into man's suffering. This joy becomes many times greater in Warren's later masterpiece, "To a

[22] Letter to Davidson, April 17, 1924; quoted by Louise Cowan in *The Fugitive Group*, 150, and printed in full in *The Literary Correspondence of Donald Davidson and Allen Tate*, 104.

Little Girl, One Year Old, in a Ruined Fortress," which contains such lines as

> Recognition explodes in delight.
> You leap like spray, or like light,

which ends with a resolution of all paradoxes, in a peace the more appreciated for the struggle by which it has been achieved:

> For fire flames but in the heart of a colder fire.
> All voice is but echo caught from a soundless voice.
> Height is not deprivation of valley, nor defect of desire.
> But defines, for the fortunate, that joy in which all joys should
>   rejoice.

In his younger years, Warren said, he was shocked by evil, but in his later years, he was shocked by good, and in such later poems as "Tell Me a Story" and "Heart of Autumn" the positive and hopeful tone outweighs the negative and despairing tone, so that the figure of the Fugitive can be seen to be fleeing less from a menacing real world than toward a visionary imagined world, symbolized by the flight of geese in both poems. In "Tell Me a Story" (the final section of *Audubon: A Vision*) he remembers hearing but not seeing their migratory flight in the spring:

> Long ago, in Kentucky, I, a boy, stood
> By a dirt road, in first dark, and heard
> The great geese hoot northward.

while in "Heart of Autumn" he is now a man, watching them again in the fall, but this time joining them in imaginative sympathy:

> and I stand, my face now lifted skyward,
> Hearing the high beat, my arms outstretched in the tingling
> Process of transformation, and soon tough legs,
>
> With folded feet, trail in the sounding vacuum of passage,
> And my heart is impacted with a fierce impulse
> To unwordable utterance—
> Toward sunset, at a great height.

Warren's career as a poet was for a long time overshadowed by his popular and critical success as a novelist, when *All the King's*

Men, perhaps the finest American political novel, won a Pulitzer Prize for Fiction in 1947, but when he won a Pulitzer Prize for Poetry with his volume *Promises* in 1957, and then another Pulitzer Prize for Poetry with *Now and Then* in 1978, his career as a poet recovered the ascendancy it had in his *Fugitive* days, and reached its apogee in 1986, shortly before his death, when he was recognized as the first official American Poet Laureate in Washington, confirming, in old age, his early fame as the youngest and most versatile of the Fugitive poets. If his early poetry held what James Dickey called "metaphysical terror," his later poetry holds "promises" of a redemptive joy.

The fame of Laura Riding as the only woman Fugitive brought her early recognition, which grew to be international by the time she published her final collection, *The Poems of Laura Riding,* in 1938, but unfortunately by then her association with Robert Graves, prompted by his admiration for her poetry through their joint appearance in *The Fugitive,* came to overshadow her poetic reputation, and the increasing literary fame of Graves, together with her own public renunciation of poetry as "a lying word," damaged her later literary career, which was not enhanced when she tried her hand at writing novels and essays. Yet when she was first published in *The Fugitive,* the editors quickly nominated her for a prize and accepted her as one of them, "a new figure in American poetry," and she responded to their encouragement, as Allen Tate reported in a letter to Davidson, "with the confession that she thinks The Fugitive is quite the equal of Poetry (and she's a competent judge, by the way) and for many reasons would prefer to appear with us."[23] She was in those days, by her own admission, "religious in my devotion to poetry," and the poems she contributed to *The Fugitive* stood out from those of the other poets because they were often written in a tightly controlled free verse like the Imagists, comparing favorably in number and quality with all the Fugitives, even Ransom, who was then at his peak as a poet. Her appealing feminine voice could be heard in the first poem they published, which was called "Dimensions," and which the Fugitives nominated for their Nashville Prize:

[23] Allen Tate to Donald Davidson, letter of 26 March 1924, in *The Literary Correspondence of Donald Davidson and Allen Tate,* p. 98.

> Measure me by myself
> And not by time or love or space
> Or beauty: Give me this last grace:

And she added vulnerability and delicacy to her voice in the lines of "Summary for Alastor":

> But finding me a shy
> And cool and quiet Eve,
> You scarcely would believe
> The fevered singer was I.

But Laura Riding's feminine identity was not without its Fugitive sense of intellectual alienation, even in these first poems, and in later poems she showed that her velvet glove held something like an iron fist, as in "Virgin of the Hills," with its defiant lines:

> The violence will be over
> And an old passion,
> Before I leave these ancient hills,
> Descend into the modern city, crying:
> Love!

It can even be said that in "The Only Daughter" Laura Riding gave a hint of the sort of witchcraft she possessed, which so attracted Robert Graves to her that he invited her to collaborate with him on *A Survey of Modernist Poetry* in 1928, and eventually made her his "White Goddess," writing a book about her fatal charm as the Muse of his poetry and fiction:

> But it is dangerous to keep an only daughter
> Like Atlantis or an isle
> Sunken in green water
> Through which may rise a smile.

Given Laura Riding's undeniable intellectual and poetic gifts, clearly demonstrated by these early Fugitive poems, it is difficult, if not impossible, to explain the motives for her later renunciation of poetry, except to guess that she took poetry too seriously for what she called its "truth-potentiality" and not seriously enough as an art, leading her to view poetry not as an end in itself but a means to an end, or, in her words, "To live in, by, for the reasons of, poetry is to habituate oneself to the good existence."[24] Whatever her reasons for renouncing poetry, after a short but happy career of only fifteen years, she chose in 1940 to pursue "the good existence" by leaving Robert Graves, her English admirer, for an American admirer, Schuyler Jackson (who as an editor of *Time* magazine had compared her with Rilke as the only true poets of the modern age), and all that can be said now is that her reputation as a poet deserves better than she herself seemed willing to grant. Her discovery as a poet by the Fugitives led to the later fame and controversy surrounding her, but her own entanglements, personal and poetic, caused her to become a somewhat forgotten figure. However, her willingness to be included in this new edition means that she will resume her rightful place among the Fugitives, and it is to be hoped that her special combination of femininity and audacity, incorporating the Fugitive theme of intellectual detachment, will win her a new generation of readers, who may come to agree with the praise she won from the editors of *The Fugitive* in the 1920's, for her "diverse play of imagination" and her "sound intellectuality and keen irony," despite all the disclaimers she later chose to make about poetry.

Beside these major figures, the minor Fugitives may seem somewhat dwarfed, yet they too have their separate strengths. Indeed, one of the most remarkable things about the group is how ably the minor Fugitives rose to the high standard set by the major ones. Merrill Moore is still foremost among them, though his productivity as a poet was so great that it became a standing joke at the meetings. He seemed to be the nearest thing to a poetry-machine, which could be turned on and off at will, and he used to amaze the group by bringing at least a dozen poems to every meeting, while the others were struggling to produce a single one. He wrote in a style that was almost instantaneous; his poems can be read about as quickly and effortlessly as a newspaper. Most of the many thousands of sonnets he wrote were not worth keeping, but by the sheer law of chance, he was bound to score a hit now and then, and he did. Stanley Johnson, Jesse Wills, and Alec Brock Stevenson were more serious and less prolific poets than

---

[24] "Original 1938 Preface To the Reader," *The Poems of Laura Riding*, A New Edition of the 1938 Collection (Manchester: Carcanet New Press, 1980), 413.

Merrill Moore, but their poetry has its own inner strengths and subtleties, which may be better appreciated in the larger representation they enjoy in this new edition, and which stand up well in comparison with the major Fugitives. Stanley Johnson published a novel called *Professor* during the Fugitive period, about a group of young professors of English at a fictitious American college who decide to bring out a little magazine, and who even think of calling it The Fugitive; it remains a light and amusing portrayal of the real Fugitive group, to which he contributed some fairly biting poems about the risks of intellectual pride. Jesse Wills published four volumes of poetry during his later years, without interrupting his highly successful career as an insurance executive in Nashville; the tone of wistful understatement about things left "Half-Said" is characteristic of his style, but he wrote a serious tribute to the Fugitives which compares with Davidson's "Lines Written for Allen Tate" in its evocation of the spirit of the early Twenties, when the group was meeting regularly near the Vanderbilt campus and publishing the magazine that lifted them from obscurity to fame. Alec Brock Stevenson was also a successful businessman, who once served as "secretary" to the Fugitives and later served as Secretary to the Vanderbilt Board of Trust, and though he never collected his poems into a volume, his individual works are marked by a powerful imagination that produced startling images, often astronomical, like "The stars are not whiter than freebooter's bones" or "The dense geometry of Pleiades," sometimes mythical, like the images in "Hemlock at Sunset" and "Icarus in November," and always brooding on final things, as in the moving sonnet newly published here, "Death, My Companion." The expansion of this edition to include the more distinguished of the outside contributors, Hart Crane and Robert Graves and John Gould Fletcher and Andrew Lytle, each of whom chose to link his fame with theirs, proves how widely poetic inspiration was shared at the time when the Fugitives worked together to create a modern Southern poetry of enduring excellence, with an outreach that proved to be international.

OXFORD, OHIO   WILLIAM PRATT
May, 1991

The Fugitive Poets

Modern Southern Poetry
in Perspective

John Crowe Ransom

BELLS FOR JOHN WHITESIDE'S DAUGHTER

There was such speed in her little body,
And such lightness in her footfall,
It is no wonder her brown study
Astonishes us all.

Her wars were bruited in our high window.
We looked among orchard trees and beyond
Where she took arms against her shadow,
Or harried unto the pond

The lazy geese, like a snow cloud
Dripping their snow on the green grass,
Tricking and stopping, sleepy and proud,
Who cried in goose, Alas,

For the tireless heart within the little
Lady with rod that made them rise
From their noon apple-dreams and scuttle
Goose-fashion under the skies!

But now go the bells, and we are ready,
In one house we are sternly stopped
To say we are vexed at her brown study,
Lying so primly propped.

DEAD BOY

The little cousin is dead, by foul subtraction,
A green bough from Virginia's aged tree,
And none of the county kin like the transaction,
Nor some of the world of outer dark, like me.

A boy not beautiful, nor good, nor clever,
A black cloud full of storms too hot for keeping,
A sword beneath his mother's heart—yet never
Woman bewept her babe as this is weeping.

A pig with a pasty face, so I had said,
Squealing for cookies, kinned by poor pretense
With a noble house. But the little man quite dead,
I see the forbears' antique lineaments.

The elder men have strode by the box of death
To the wide flag porch, and muttering low send round
The bruit of the day. O friendly waste of breath!
Their hearts are hurt with a deep dynastic wound.

He was pale and little, the foolish neighbors say;
The first-fruits, saith the Preacher, the Lord hath taken;
But this was the old tree's late branch wrenched away,
Grieving the sapless limbs, the shorn and shaken.

THE VANITY OF THE BLUE GIRLS

Twirling your blue skirts, traveling the sward
Under the towers of your seminary,
Go listen to your teachers old and contrary
Without believing a word.

Tie the white fillets then about your hair
And think no more of what will come to pass
Than bluebirds that go walking on the grass
And chattering on the air.

Practise your beauty, blue girls, before it fail;
And I will cry with my loud lips and publish
Beauty which all our power shall never establish,
It is so frail.

For I could tell you a story which is true;
I know a lady with a terrible tongue,
Blear eyes fallen from blue,
All her perfections tarnished—yet it is not long
Since she was lovelier than any of you.

THE VANITY OF THE BRIGHT YOUNG MEN*

Grim in my tight black coat as the sleazy beetle
But never minding my looks,
A boy removed, reported not liking people,
A familiar only to books;

Going alone to assembly but always pushing
Even to say my prayers,
Glaring with cold grey eyes at whom I was brushing
Who would if they could with theirs;

But walking afternoons in our green forest
And wasting for my miracle
Should a blackbird sit on my arm and mutter the barest
Prelude to a mighty oracle;

Passing once by luck of my chances and choices
Under those Druid trees
Whose leaves were ears and tongues translating voices
Stitched in the wind's wheeze;

Against me the counsels of spirits not being darkened
But talking each to each
Till I slowed my stride in the shrubbery and hearkened
Unto phrases of English speech;

One saying, "This boy who tugs at the tether is other
Than he and they suppose"—
But one, "Yet sired and dammed by a father and mother
And surely acknowledges those?"—

* New version of a poem once known as "Tom, Tom the Piper's Son."

A third, "Suppose our man was a changeling but knows not
Yet bears himself as a Prince"—
"Of a far kingdom and should return but goes not?"—
"Fifteen long winters since"—

But like a King and subject to a King's condition
I towered and marched right on
Not stooping to eavesdrop even for revelation,
And quick that talk was gone,

And prompt I showed as the bell's last throb appointed
In the loud and litten room
Unhailed by the love that leaps to the Heir Anointed,
"Hush, O hush, he is come!"

CONRAD IN TWILIGHT

Conrad, Conrad, aren't you old
To sit so late in your mouldy garden?
And I think Conrad knows it well,
Nursing his knees, too rheumy and cold
To warm the wraith of a Forest of Arden.

Neuralgia in the back of his neck,
His lungs filling with such miasma,
His feet dipping in leafage and muck:
Conrad! you've forgotten asthma.

Conrad's house has thick red walls,
The log on Conrad's hearth is blazing,
Slippers and pipe and tea are served,
Butter and toast are meant for pleasing!
Still Conrad's back is not uncurved
And here's an autumn on him, teasing.

Autumn days in our section
Are the most used-up thing on earth
(Or in the waters under the earth)
Having no more color nor predilection
Than cornstalks too wet for the fire,
A ribbon rotting on the byre,
A man's face as weathered as straw
By the summer's flare and winter's flaw.

NECROLOGICAL

The friar had said his paternosters duly
And scourged his limbs, and afterwards would have slept;
But with much riddling his head became unruly,
He arose, from the quiet monastery he crept.

Dawn lightened the place where the battle had been won.
The people were dead—it is easy he thought to die—
These dead remained, but the living all were gone,
Gone with the wailing trumps of victory.

The dead wore no raiment against the air,
Bartholomew's men had spoiled them where they fell;
In defeat the heroes' bodies were whitely bare,
The field was white like meads of asphodel.

Not all were white; some gory and fabulous
Whom the sword had pierced and then the grey wolf eaten;
But the brother reasoned that heroes' flesh was thus.
Flesh fails, and the postured bones lie weather-beaten.

The lords of chivalry lay prone and shattered.
The gentle and the bodyguard of yeomen;
Bartholomew's stroke went home—but little it mattered,
Batholomew went to be stricken of other foemen.

Beneath the blue ogive of the firmament
Was a dead warrior, clutching whose mighty knees
Was a leman, who with her flame had warmed his tent,
For him enduring all men's pleasantries.

Close by the sable stream that purged the plain
Lay the white stallion and his rider thrown,
The great beast had spilled there his little brain,
And the little groin of the knight was spilled by a stone.

The youth possessed him then of a crooked blade
Deep in the belly of a lugubrious wight;
He fingered it well, and it was cunningly made;
But strange apparatus was it for a Carmelite.

Then he sat upon a hill and bowed his head
As under a riddle, and in a deep surmise
So still that he likened himself unto those dead
Whom the kites of Heaven solicited with sweet cries.

JANET WAKING

Beautifully Janet slept
Till it was deeply morning. She woke then
And thought about her dainty-feathered hen,
To see how it had kept.

One kiss she gave her mother.
Only a small one gave she to her daddy
Who would have kissed each curl of his shining baby;
No kiss at all for her brother.

"Old Chucky, old Chucky!" she cried,
Running across the world upon the grass
To Chucky's house, and listening. But alas,
Her Chucky had died.

It was a transmogrifying bee
Came droning down on Chucky's old bald head
And sat and put the poison. It scarcely bled,
But how exceedingly

And purply did the knot
Swell with the venom and communicate
Its rigor! Now the poor comb stood up straight
But Chucky did not.

So there was Janet
Kneeling on the wet grass, crying her brown hen
(Translated far beyond the daughters of men)
To rise and walk upon it.

And weeping fast as she had breath
Janet implored us, "Wake her from her sleep!"
And would not be instructed in how deep
Was the forgetful kingdom of death.

PIAZZA PIECE

—I am a gentleman in a dustcoat trying
To make you hear. Your ears are soft and small
And listen to an old man not at all,
They want the young men's whispering and sighing.
But see the roses on your trellis dying
And hear the spectral singing of the moon;
For I must have my lovely lady soon,
I am a gentleman in a dustcoat trying.

—I am a lady young in beauty waiting
Until my truelove comes, and then we kiss.
But what grey man among the vines is this
Whose words are dry and faint as in a dream?
Back from my trellis, Sir, before I scream!
I am a lady young in beauty waiting.

OLD MANSION

As an intruder I trudged with careful innocence
To mask in decency a meddlesome stare,
Passing the old house often on its eminence,
Exhaling my foreign weed on its weighted air.

Here age seemed newly imaged for the historian
After his monstrous châteaux on the Loire,
A beauty not for depicting by old vulgarian
Reiterations which gentle readers abhor.

Each time of seeing I absorbed some other feature
Of a house whose legend could in no wise be brief
Nor ignoble, for it expired as sweetly as Nature,
With her tinge of oxidation on autumn leaf.

It was a Southern manor. One need hardly imagine
Towers, white monoliths, or even ivied walls;
But sufficient state if its peacock *was* a pigeon;
Where no courts held, but grave rites and funerals.

Indeed, not distant, possibly not external
To the property, were tombstones, where the catafalque
Had carried their dead; and projected a note too charnel
But for the honeysuckle on its intricate stalk.

Stability was the character of its rectangle
Whose line was seen in part and guessed in part
Through trees. Decay was the tone of old brick and shingle.
Green blinds dragging frightened the watchful heart

To assert: "Your mansion, long and richly inhabited,
Its exits and entrances suiting the children of man,
Will not forever be thus, O man, exhibited,
And one had best hurry to enter it if one can."

And at last with my happier angel's own temerity,
Did I clang their brazen knocker against the door,
To beg their dole of a look, in simple charity,
Or crumbs of history dropping from their great store.

But it came to nothing—and may so gross denial,
Which has been deplored duly with a beating of the breast,
Never shorten the tired historian, loyal
To acknowledge defeat and discover a new quest—

The old mistress was ill, and sent my dismissal
By one even more wrappered and lean and dark
Than that warped concierge and imperturbable vassal
Who bids you begone from her master's Gothic park.

Emphatically, the old house crumbled; the ruins
Would litter, as already the leaves, this petted sward;
And no annalist went in to the lord or the peons;
The antiquary would finger the bits of shard.

But on retreating I saw myself in the token,
How loving from my foreign weed the feather curled
On the languid air; and I went with courage shaken
To dip, alas, into some unseemlier world.

PHILOMELA

Procne, Philomela, and Itylus,
Your names are liquid, your improbable tale
Is recited in the classic numbers of the nightingale.
Ah, but our numbers are not felicitous,
It goes not liquidly for us.

Perched on a Roman ilex, and duly apostrophized,
The nightingale descanted unto Ovid;
She has even appeared to the Teutons, the swilled and gravid;
At Fontainebleau it may be the bird was gallicized;
Never was she baptized.

To England came Philomela with her pain,
Fleeing the hawk her husband; querulous ghost,
She wanders when he sits heavy on his roost,
Utters herself in the original again,
The untranslatable refrain.

Not to these shores she came! this other Thrace,
Environ barbarous to the royal Attic;
How could her delicate dirge run democratic,
Delivered in a cloudless boundless public place
To an inordinate race?

I pernoctated with the Oxford students once,
And in the quadrangles, in the cloisters, on the Cher,
Precociously knocked at antique doors ajar,
Fatuously touched the hems of the hierophants,
Sick of my dissonance.

I went out to Bagley Wood, I climbed the hill;
Even the moon had slanted off in a twinkling,
I heard the sepulchral owl and a few bells tinkling,
There was no more villainous day to unfulfil,
The diuturnity was still.

Up from the darkest wood where Philomela sat,
Her fairy numbers issued. What then ailed me?
My ears are called capacious but they failed me,
Her classics registered a little flat!
I rose, and venomously spat.

Philomela, Philomela, lover of song,
I am in despair if we may make us worthy,
A bantering breed sophistical and swarthy;
Unto more beautiful, persistently more young,
Thy fabulous provinces belong.

AMPHIBIOUS CROCODILE

In due season the amphibious crocodile
Rose from the waves and clambered on the bank
And clothed himself, having cleansed his toes which stank
Of bayous of Florida and estuaries of Nile.

And if he had had not water on his brain,
Remember what joys were his. The complete landlubber
In a green mackintosh and overshoes of rubber—
Putting his umbrella up against the rain

For fear of the influenza—sleeking his curls—
Prowling among the petticoats and the teacups—
Visiting the punchbowl to the verge of hiccups—
Breaching his promises and playing with the girls.

At length in grey spats he must cross the ocean.
So this is Paris? Lafayette, we are here.
Bring us sweet wines but none of your French beer.
And he weeps on Notre Dame with proper emotion.

This is the Rive Gauche, this is the Hotel Crillon.
Where are the brave poilus? They are slain by his French.
And suddenly he cries, I want to see a trench!
Up in the North eventually he finds one

Which is all green slime and water; whereupon lewd
Nostalgic tremors assail him; with strangled oaths
He flees; he would be kicking off his clothes
And reverting to his pre-Christian mother's nude.

Next on the grand tour is Westminster, and Fleet Street.
His Embassy must present him to King George.
Who is the gentleman whose teeth are so large?
That is Mr. Crocodile the renowned aesthete.

To know England really one must try the country
And the week-end parties; he is persuaded to straddle
A yellow beast in a red coat on a flat saddle.
Much too gymnastical are the English gentry.

Surely a Scotch and soda with the Balliol men.
But when old Crocodile rises to speak at the Union
He is too miserably conscious of his bunion
And toes too large for the aesthetic regimen.

It is too too possible he has wandered far
From the simple center of his rugged nature.
I wonder, says he, if I am the sort of creature
To live by projects, travel, affaires de coeur?

Crocodile ponders the marrying of a wife,
She has a ready-made fortune and ready-made family;
The lady is not a poem but she is a homily,
But he hates the rectangular charms of the virtuous life.

Soberly Crocodile sips of the Eucharist.
But as he meditates the obscene complexes
And infinite involutions of the sexes,
Crocodile sets up for a pyscho-analyst.

Great is his learning. He learns to discuss
Pure being, both the Who's Who and What's What,
Affirms that A is A, refutes that B is not.
This is a clean life without mud and muss.

But who would ever have thought it took such strength
To whittle the tree of being to a point
While the deep-sea urge cries Largo, and every joint
Tingles with gross desire of lying at length?

Of all the elements mixed in Crocodile
Water is principal; but water flows
By paths of least resistance; and water goes
Down, down, down; which is too infantile.

The earth spins from its poles, and is glared on
By the fierce incessant suns, but here is news
For a note in the fine-print column of the Thursday Reviews:
Old Robert Crocodile is packed up and gone.

His dear friends cannot find him. The ladies write
As usual but their lavender notes are returned
By the U.S. Postmaster and secretively burned.
He has mysteriously gone out of sight.

Crocodile hangs his pretty clothes on a limb
And lies with his fathers, and with his mothers too,
And his brothers and sisters as it seems right to do;
The family religion is good enough for him.

Full length he lies and goes as water goes,
He weeps for joy and welters in the flood,
Floating he lies extended many a rood,
And quite invisible but for the end of his nose.

CAPTAIN CARPENTER

Captain Carpenter rose up in his prime
Put on his pistols and went riding out
But had got wellnigh nowhere at that time
Till he fell in with ladies in a rout.

It was a pretty lady and all her train
That played with him so sweetly but before
An hour she'd taken a sword with all her main
And twined him of his nose for evermore.

Captain Carpenter mounted up one day
And rode straightway into a stranger rogue
That looked unchristian but be that as may
The Captain did not wait upon prologue.

But drew upon him out of his great heart
The other swung against him with a club
And cracked his two legs at the shinny part
And let him roll and stick like any tub.

Captain Carpenter rode many a time
From male and female took he sundry harms
He met the wife of Satan crying "I'm
The she-wolf bids you shall bear no more arms."

Their strokes and counters whistled in the wind
I wish he had delivered half his blows
But where she should have made off like a hind
The bitch bit off his arms at the elbows.

And Captain Carpenter parted with his ears
To a black devil that used him in this wise
O Jesus ere his threescore and ten years
Another had plucked out his sweet blue eyes.

Captain Carpenter got up on his roan
And sallied from the gate in hell's despite
I heard him asking in the grimmest tone
If any enemy yet there was to fight?

"To any adversary it is fame
If he risk to be wounded by my tongue
Or burnt in two beneath my red heart's flame
Such are the perils he is cast among.

"But if he can he has a pretty choice
From an anatomy with little to lose
Whether he cut my tongue and take my voice
Or whether it be my round red heart he choose."

It was the neatest knave that ever was seen
Stepping in perfume from his lady's bower
Who at this word put in his merry mien
And fell on Captain Carpenter like a tower.

I would not knock old fellows in the dust
But there lay Captain Carpenter on his back
His weapons were the old heart in his bust
And a blade shook between rotten teeth alack.

The rogue in scarlet and grey soon knew his mind
He wished to get his trophy and depart
With gentle apology and touch refined
He pierced him and produced the Captain's heart.

God's mercy rest on Captain Carpenter now
I thought him Sirs an honest gentleman
Citizen husband soldier and scholar enow
Let jangling kites eat of him if they can.

But God's deep curses follow after those
That shore him of his goodly nose and ears
His legs and strong arms at the two elbows
And eyes that had not watered seventy years.

The curse of hell upon the sleek upstart
That got the Captain finally on his back
And took the red red vitals of his heart
And made the kites to whet their beaks clack clack.

THE EQUILIBRISTS

Full of her long white arms and milky skin
He had a thousand times remembered sin.
Alone in the press of people traveled he,
Minding her jacinth, and myrrh, and ivory.

Mouth he remembered: the quaint orifice
From which came heat that flamed upon the kiss,
Till cold words came down spiral from the head.
Grey doves from the officious tower illsped.

Body: it was a white field ready for love,
On her body's field, with the gaunt tower above,
The lilies grew, beseeching him to take,
If he would pluck and wear them, bruise and break.

Eyes talking: Never mind the cruel words,
Embrace my flowers, but not embrace the swords.
But what they said, the doves came straightway flying
And unsaid: Honor, Honor, they came crying.

Importunate her doves. Too pure, too wise,
Clambering on his shoulder, saying, Arise,
Leave me now, and never let us meet,
Eternal distance now command thy feet.

Predicament indeed, which thus discovers
Honor among thieves, Honor between lovers.
O such a little word is Honor, they feel!
But the grey word is between them cold as steel.

At length I saw these lovers fully were come
Into their torture of equilibrium;
Dreadfully had forsworn each other, and yet
They were bound each to each, and they did not forget.

And rigid as two painful stars, and twirled
About the clustered night their prison world,
They burned with fierce love always to come near,
But honor beat them back and kept them clear.

Ah, the strict lovers, they are ruined now!
I cried in anger. But with puddled brow
Devising for those gibbeted and brave
Came I descanting: Man, what would you have?

For spin your period out, and draw your breath,
A kinder saeculum begins with Death.
Would you ascend to Heaven and bodiless dwell?
Or take your bodies honorless to Hell?

In Heaven you have heard no marriage is,
No white flesh tinder to your lecheries,
Your male and female tissue sweetly shaped
Sublimed away, and furious blood escaped.

Great lovers lie in Hell, the stubborn ones
Infatuate of the flesh upon the bones;
Stuprate, they rend each other when they kiss,
The pieces kiss again, no end to this.

But still I watched them spinning, orbited nice.
Their flames were not more radiant than their ice.
I dug in the quiet earth and wrought the tomb
And made these lines to memorize their doom:—

EPITAPH

Equilibrists lie here; stranger, tread light;
Close, but untouching in each other's sight;
Mouldered the lips and ashy the tall skull.
Let them lie perilous and beautiful.

PAINTED HEAD

By dark severance the apparition head
Smiles from the air a capital on no
Column or a Platonic perhaps head
On a canvas sky depending from nothing;

Stirs up an old illusion of grandeur
By tickling the instinct of heads to be
Absolute and to try decapitation
And to play truant from the body bush;

But too happy and beautiful for those sorts
Of head (homekeeping heads are happiest)
Discovers maybe thirty unwidowed years
Of not dishonoring the faithful stem;

Is nameless and has authored for the evil
Historian headhunters neither book
Nor state and is therefore distinct from tart
Heads with crowns and guilty gallery heads;

Wherefore the extravagant device of art
Unhousing by abstraction this once head
Was capital irony by a loving hand
That knew the no treason of a head like this;

Makes repentance in an unlovely head
For having vinegarly traduced the flesh
Till, the hurt flesh recusing, the hard egg
Is shrunken to its own deathlike surface;

And an image thus. The body bears the head
(So hardly one they terribly are two)
Feeds and obeys and unto please what end?
Not to the glory of tyrant head but to

The estate of body. Beauty is of body.
The flesh contouring shallowly on a head
Is a rock-garden needing body's love
And best bodiness to colorify

The big blue birds sitting and sea-shell flats
And caves, and on the iron acropolis
To spread the hyacinthine hair and rear
The olive garden for the nightingales.

ANTIQUE HARVESTERS

(SCENE: *Of the Mississippi the bank sinister,
and of the Ohio the bank sinister.*)

Tawny are the leaves turned but they still hold,
And it is harvest; what shall this land produce?
A meager hill of kernels, a runnel of juice;
Declension looks from our land, it is old.
Therefore let us assemble, dry, grey, spare,
And mild as yellow air.

"I hear the croak of a raven's funeral wing."
The young men would be joying in the song
Of passionate birds; their memories are not long.
What is it thus rehearsed in sable? "Nothing."
Trust not but the old endure, and shall be older
Than the scornful beholder.

We pluck the spindling ears and gather the corn.
One spot has special yield? "On this spot stood
Heroes and drenched it with their only blood."
And talk meets talk, as echoes from the horn
Of the hunter—echoes are the old man's arts,
Ample are the chambers of their hearts.

Here come the hunters, keepers of a rite;
The horn, the hounds, the lank mares coursing by
Straddled with archetypes of chivalry;
And the fox, lovely ritualist, in flight
Offering his unearthly ghost to quarry;
And the fields, themselves to harry.

Resume, harvesters. The treasure is full bronze
Which you will garner for the Lady, and the moon
Could tinge it no yellower than does this noon;
But grey will quench it shortly—the field, men, stones.
Pluck fast, dreamers; prove as you amble slowly
Not less than men, not wholly.

Bare the arm, dainty youths, bend the knees
Under bronze burdens. And by an autumn tone
As by a grey, as by a green, you will have known
Your famous Lady's image; for so have these;
And if one say that easily will your hands
More prosper in other lands,

Angry as wasp-music be your cry then:
"Forsake the Proud Lady, of the heart of fire,
The look of snow, to the praise of a dwindled choir,
Song of degenerate specters that were men?
The sons of the fathers shall keep her, worthy of
What these have done in love."

True, it is said of our Lady, she ageth.
But see, if you peep shrewdly, she hath not stooped;
Take no thought of her servitors that have drooped,
For we are nothing; and if one talk of death—
Why, the ribs of the earth subsist frail as a breath
If but God wearieth.

Stanley Johnson

AN INTELLECTUAL'S FUNERAL

On such a day we put him in a box
And carried him to that last house, the grave;
All round the people walked upon the streets
Without once thinking that he had gone.
Their hard heels clacked upon the pavement stones.

A voiceless change had muted all his thoughts
To a deep significance we could not know;
And yet we knew that he knew all at last.
We heard with grave wonder the falling clods,
And with grave wonder met the loud day.

The night would come and day, but we had died.
With new green sod the melancholy gate
Was closed and locked, and we went pitiful.
Our clacking heels upon the pavement stones
Did knock and knock for Death to let us in.

A SONNET OF THE YELLOW LEAF

Green bend the poplar trees by Cumberland,
And skyward lift white arms of sycamore;
And there we walked upon the meager sand
While fast behind us summer closed the door.

I analysed the wreckage of the year—
The smitten leaf, the leering buck-eye's burial,
Your drooping cheeks; when, lo, down there
The river brought misfortunate memorial:

I saw within the jesting water's marge
Your soft young face blur out with age, and after
Come wrinkles in the mirror's quiet surge,
To move the poplar leaves and me to laughter.

But terror favored your stare like the grey stone,
A tremor shook you, you wept, and the glory was gone.

TO A PARK SWAN

I caught your shadow in the deep pool,
A naked sword of beauty in the dark.
And I had read of the white swans at Coole,
And heard the printed voice of the skylark.

The skies were lifted quick from this dull place;
Like Lohengrin I heard a silver bell.
I saw the maiden Leda's neat disgrace;
My vision beat historic wings—and fell.

For what of the albatross and the wild swan,
Skirting a black sea patch on a salty morn,
While I stand empty—and the voices are gone—
And you cram peanuts and the white popcorn.

I have not known the swan song, though my prayer
Has beat with cygnet wings no slight emotion
To find inanity itself astare,
A goitered goose upon a festered ocean.

And what of Eve, Semiramis, and Sappho?
It is enough—the tale brings tragic hush.
There was a time—but it was long ago!
Perhaps old Moses saw the burning bush.

Donald Davidson

UTTERANCE

I am not what my lips explain,
   And more devotedly inclined
Than these dry sentences reveal
   That break in crude shards from my mind.

What way is there of gesturing
   The cruelly impounded thought?
It comes, it pierces me like steel,
   It flames, but I can utter naught.

The soul, so struggling to upheave
   Its changeful self, the wistful me,
Is caught in labyrinthean ways
   And tangled irrevocably.

And am I worth the guess you make?
   O fact so digged in circumstance!
It surely is not known to me,
   And you must take my Self on chance.

LINES FOR A TOMB

Recite the dangers chiselled on this face:
How I was clipped by scorn and maimed by lies;
How conscience hedged my soul; law chilled my eyes;
      Ropes cut my grace.

Recite therewith the flame of victories:
How out of blood and dust I gathered mirth;
And was content to find in flesh and earth
      Strange ecstasies.

But most recite what made me captive here,
Weighted with stone, wrapped in a sluggard's peace,
And ask of men if this is God's release
      Or only his fear.

REDIVIVUS

Thin lips can make a music;
Hateful eyes can see;
Crooked limbs go dancing
To a strange melody.

The probing knife of madness
Can start a dullard brain.
Cold cheeks can feel kisses
And warm with tears again.

The surly heart of clowns
Can crack with ecstasy;
Rootbound oaks toss limbs
If winds come fervently.

Then let my skeleton soul
Writhe upward from the loam,
Drink red morning again,
And look gently home.

LEE IN THE MOUNTAINS
1865-1870

Walking into the shadows, walking alone
Where the sun falls through the ruined boughs of locust
Up to the president's office. . . .
                                        Hearing the voices
Whisper, *Hush, it is General Lee!* And strangely
Hearing my own voice say, *Good morning, boys.*
(*Don't get up. You are early. It is long*
Before the bell. You will have long to wait
On these cold steps. . . .)
                                  The young have time to wait
But soldiers' faces under their tossing flags
Lift no more by any road or field,
And I am spent with old wars and new sorrow.
Walking the rocky path, where steps decay
And the paint cracks and grass eats on the stone.
It is not General Lee, young men . . .
It is Robert Lee in a dark civilian suit who walks,
An outlaw fumbling for the latch, a voice
Commanding in a dream where no flag flies.

My father's house is taken and his hearth
Left to the candle-drippings where the ashes
Whirl at a chimney-breath on the cold stone.
I can hardly remember my father's look, I cannot
Answer his voice as he calls farewell in the misty
Mounting where riders gather at gates.
He was old then—I was a child—his hand
Held out for mine, some daybreak snatched away,
And he rode out, a broken man. Now let
His lone grave keep, surer than cypress roots,
The vow I made beside him. God too late
Unseals to certain eyes the drift
Of time and the hopes of men and a sacred cause.
The fortune of the Lees goes with the land
Whose sons will keep it still. My mother

Told me much. She sat among the candles,
Fingering the *Memoirs*, now so long unread.
And as my pen moves on across the page
Her voice comes back, a murmuring distillation
Of old Virginia times now faint and gone,
The hurt of all that was and cannot be.

Why did my father write? I know he saw
History clutched as a wraith out of blowing mist
Where tongues are loud, and a glut of little souls
Laps at the too much blood and the burning house
He would have his say, but I shall not have mine.
What I do is only a son's devoir
To a lost father. Let him only speak.
The rest must pass to men who never knew
(But on a written page) the strike of armies,
And never heard the long Confederate cry
Charge through the muzzling smoke or saw the bright
Eyes of the beardless boys go up to death.
It is Robert Lee who writes with his father's hand—
The rest must go unsaid and the lips be locked.

If all were told, as it cannot be told—
If all the dread opinion of the heart
Now could speak, now in the shame and torment
Lashing the bound and trampled States—

If a word were said, as it cannot be said—

I see clear waters run in Virginia's Valley
And in the house the weeping of young women
Rises no more. The waves of grain begin.
The Shenandoah is golden with new grain.
The Blue Ridge, crowned with a haze of light,
Thunders no more. The horse is at plough. The rifle
Returns to the chimney crotch and the hunter's hand.
And nothing else than this? Was it for this
That on an April day we stacked our arms
Obedient to a soldier's trust? To lie
Ground by heels of little men,

Forever maimed, defeated, lost, impugned?
And was I then betrayed? Did I betray?
If it were said, as still it might be said—
If it were said, and a word should run like fire,
Like living fire into the roots of grass,
The sunken flag would kindle on wild hills,
The brooding hearts would waken, and the dream
Stir like a crippled phantom under the pines,
And this torn earth would quicken into shouting
Beneath the feet of ragged bands—
                                    The pen
Turns to the waiting page, the sword
Bows to the rust that cankers and the silence.

Among these boys whose eyes lift up to mine
Within gray walls where droning wasps repeat
A hollow reveillé, I still must face,
Day after day, the courier with his summons
Once more to surrender, now to surrender all.
Without arms or men I stand, but with knowledge only
I face what long I saw, before others knew,
When Pickett's men streamed back, and I heard the tangled
Cry of the Wilderness wounded, bloody with doom.

The mountains, once I said, in the little room
At Richmond, by the huddled fire, but still
The President shook his head. The mountains wait,
I said, in the long beat and rattle of siege
At cratered Petersburg. Too late
We sought the mountains and those people came.
And Lee is in mountains now, beyond Appomattox,
Listening long for voices that never will speak
Again; hearing the hoofbeats come and go and fade
Without a stop, without a brown hand lifting
The tent-flap, or a bugle call at dawn,
Or ever on the long white road the flag
Of Jackson's quick brigades. I am alone,
Trapped, consenting, taken at last in mountains.

It is not the bugle now, or the long roll beating.
The simple stroke of a chapel bell forbids
The hurtling dream, recalls the lonely mind.
Young men, the God of your fathers is a just
And merciful God Who in this blood once shed
On your green altars measures out all days,
And measures out the grace
Whereby alone we live;
And in His might He waits,
Brooding within the certitude of time,
To bring this lost forsaken valor
And the fierce faith undying
And the love quenchless
To flower among the hills to which we cleave,
To fruit upon the mountains whither we flee,
Never forsaking, never denying
His children and His children's children forever
Unto all generations of the faithful heart.

SEQUEL OF APPOMATTOX

A whisper flies to the empty sleeve
Pinned on the braidless coat,
And a rumor flushes the scarred young cheek
Of a man in butternut.

The riders go past fenceless fields.
They meet by the ruined wall.
And the gaunt horses crop and stray
While voices mutter and drawl.

The crow starts from the blackberry bush,
But the windowless house won't tell.
Darkness watches the ravished gate.
No hand swings the fallen bell.

Till roads are white with columns
Of phantom cavalry
That move as by the dead's cool will
Without guns or infantry.

And the hoofbeats of many horsemen
Stop and call from the grave:
Remember, I was your master;
Remember, you were my slave.

At midnight a town's four corners
Wake to the whistles' keening;
The march of the dead is a long march.
Certain its meaning.

Something for grandfathers to tell
Boys who clamor and climb.
And were you there, and did you ride
With the men of that old time?

TWILIGHT ON UNION STREET

In the cool of morning Andrew Jackson came,
A young man riding on a horse of flame,
Tossed the reins to a black boy, and strode
High-booted and quick-oathed to court and code.

Of a sultry noontime General Jackson stalked,
A grimness that put silence where men talked.
The fluttering of the gossips thinned and fled;
They knew where General Jackson left his dead.

And now the twilight. History grows dim.
The traffic leads, we no more follow him;
In bronze he rides, saluting James K. Polk,
His horse's rump turned to us in the smoke.

ON A REPLICA OF THE PARTHENON

Why do they come? What do they seek
Who build but never read their Greek?
The classic stillness of a pool
Beleaguered in its certitude
By aimless motors that can make
Only incertainty more sure;
And where the willows crowd the pure
Expanse of clouds and blue that stood
Around the gables Athens wrought,
Shop-girls embrace a plaster thought,
And eye Poseidon's loins ungirt,
And never heed the brandished spear
Or feel the bright-eyed maiden's rage
Whose gaze the sparrows violate;
But the sky drips its spectral dirt,
And gods, like men, to soot revert.
Gone is the mild, the serene air.
The golden years are come too late.
Pursue not wisdom or virtue here,
But what blind motion, what dim last
Regret of men who slew their past
Raised up this bribe against their fate.

RANDALL, MY SON

Randall, my son, before you came just now
I saw the lean vine fingering at the latch,
And through the rain I heard the poplar bough
Thresh at the blinds it never used to touch,
And I was old and troubled overmuch,
And called in the deep night, but there was none
To comfort me or answer, Randall, my son.

But mount the stair and lay you down till morn.
The bed is made—the lamp is burning low.
Within the changeless room where you were born
I wait the changing day when you must go.
I am unreconciled to what I know,
And I am old with questions never done
That will not let me slumber, Randall, my son.

Randall, my son, I cannot hear the cries
That lure beyond familiar fields, or see
The glitter of the world that draws your eyes.
Cold is the mistress that beckons you from me.
I wish her sleek hunting might never come to be—
For in our woods where deer and fox still run
An old horn blows at daybreak, Randall, my son.

And tell me then, will you some day bequeath
To your own son not born or yet begotten,
The lustre of a sword that sticks in sheath,
A house that crumbles and a fence that's rotten?
Take, what I leave, your own land unforgotten;
Hear, what I hear, in a far chase new begun
An old horn's husky music, Randall, my son.

SANCTUARY

You must remember this when I am gone,
And tell your sons—for you will have tall sons,
And times will come when answers will not wait.
Remember this: if ever defeat is black
Upon your eyelids, go to the wilderness
In the dread last of trouble, for your foe
Tangles there, more than you, and paths are strange
To him, that are your paths, in the wilderness,
And were your fathers' paths, and once were mine.

You must remember this, and mark it well
As I have told it—what my eyes have seen
And where my feet have walked beyond forgetting.
But tell it not often, tell it only at last
When your sons know what blood runs in their veins.
And when the danger comes, as come it will,
Go as your fathers went with woodsman's eyes
Uncursed, unflinching, studying only the path.

First, what you cannot carry, burn or hide.
Leave nothing here for *him* to take or eat.
Bury, perhaps, what you can surely find
If good chance ever bring you back again.
Level the crops. Take only what you need:
A little corn for an ash-cake, a little
Side-meat for your three days' wilderness ride.
Horses for your women and your children,
And one to lead, if you should have that many.
Then go. At once. Do not wait until
You see *his* great dust rising in the valley.
Then it will be too late.
Go when you hear that he has crossed Will's Ford.
Others will know and pass the word to you—
A tap on the blinds, a hoot-owl's cry at dusk.

Do not look back. You can see your roof afire
When you reach high ground. Yet do not look.
Do not turn. Do not look back.
Go further on. Go high. Go deep.
The line of this rail-fence east across the old-fields
Leads to the cane-bottoms. Back of that,
A white-oak tree beside a spring, the one
Chopped with three blazes on the hillward side.
There pick up the trail. I think it was
A buffalo path once or an Indian road.
You follow it three days along the ridge
Until you reach the spruce woods. Then a cliff
Breaks, where the trees are thickest, and you look
Into a cove, and right across, Chilhowee
Is suddenly there, and you are home at last.
Sweet springs of mountain water in that cove
Run always. Deer and wild turkey range.
Your kin, knowing the way, long there before you
Will have good fires and kettles on to boil,
Bough-shelters reared and thick beds of balsam.
There in tall timber you will be as free
As were your fathers once when Tryon raged
In Carolina hunting Regulators,
Or Tarleton rode to hang the old-time Whigs.
Some tell how in that valley young Sam Houston
Lived long ago with his brother, Oo-loo-te-ka,
Reading Homer among the Cherokee;
And others say a Spaniard may have found it
Far from De Soto's wandering turned aside,
And left his legend on a boulder there.
And some that this was a sacred place to all
Old Indian tribes before the Cherokee
Came to our eastern mountains. Men have found
Images carved in bird-shapes there and faces
Moulded into the great kind look of gods.

These old tales are like prayers. I only know
This is the secret refuge of our race
Told only from a father to his son,
A trust laid on your lips, as though a vow
To generations past and yet to come.
There, from the bluffs above, you may at last
Look back to all you left, and trace
His dust and flame, and plan your harrying
If you would gnaw his ravaging flank, or smite
Him in his glut among the smouldering ricks.
Or else, forgetting ruin, you may lie
On sweet grass by a mountain stream, to watch
The last wild eagle soar or the last raven
Cherish his brood within their rocky nest,
Or see, when mountain shadows first grow long,
The last enchanted white deer come to drink.

HERMITAGE

Written in Memory of Andrew Davidson, A Pioneer of Southwest Virginia and of Bedford County, Tennessee

I. DESCENDING CHESTNUT RIDGE

Now let my habitude be where the vine
Tumbles the sagging rails, and the late crow
Alone can challenge, whom for countersign
I open these uncrafty hands,
Unweaponed now, to seek upon the hill
Stones where no filial tribute can be lost,
Above the bones not laid in stranger's lands,
But their own earth commingles with their dust;

To say for what beholden, to fulfill
The unuttered vows;

To hear the great wind in the twilight boughs
Whirl down the sapless nations and the cold
Fix their long-withering moment which conceives
No more the great year that their dreams foretold;

To walk where autumn heaps their promises
And, unregenerate by false faith, to tread
World-gazing prophecies as leaves to leaves;

To let the sibylline fragments fly;

Then slow descending by the hidden road
To mark the clearing and to know the hearth
Where one smoke stands against the frosty sky
And one axe rings above the frosty earth.

II. THE IMMIGRANT

I cannot see him plain, that far-off sire
Who notched the first oak on this western hill,
And the bronze tablet cannot tell what fire

—Urging the deep bone back to the viking wave—
Kindled his immigrant eye and drove his will.
But in the hearthside tale his rumor grows
As voice to voice into the folk-chain melts
And clamor of danger brings the lost kin close.

The runes run on, the song links stave by stave.
I summon him, the man of flints and pelts,
Alert with gun and axe. The valley-rim
Uplifts the wanderer on the buffalo-path,
First of the host of all who came like him,
Harried from croft and chapel, glen and strath.

Now where the beech-mast falls, no pibrochs wail.
The claymore rusts forgetting once how red
The dew lay at Culloden. Old feuds fail,
And nevermore the axe sings on the wall—
Since age on age we fled,
Since we together, Gael and Gaul,
Palatine, Huguenot, came in company
And washed the old bitter wars in the salt sea.

III. IN BLUE-STOCKING HOLLOW

Traveler, rest. The time of man runs on;
Our home is far across the western wave
Back of whose steeps, forsaken and foregone,
Lost continents ebb we have no power to save.
The unending cycle breaks against this strand
Where blue tidewater laps our greener land.

And once the Virginian voyage brings us clear,
The hoodless eagles of the new-world skies
Towering, unshackle us, and the numberless deer
Confound the musket, and the wild geese rise,
Hurling southward with invincible wing
Omens unriddled for our journeying.

Rough pilgrims, faring far, whose Hesperus
Stooped by the piney woods or mountain cove,
Or whom the Buffalo Gods to the perilous
Lift of the Great Divide and the redwood grove
Spoke on and bid lay down from sea to sea
The sill and hearthstone of our destiny.

Salving our wounds, from the moody kings we came,
And even while kinsmen's shoulders raised and set
The first log true, bethought us of a name
To seal the firm lips of our unregret,
To charm the door against the former age
And bless the lintel of our hermitage.

Recite then while the inviolate hearth-flame leaps
How Ilion fell, and, hound at knee, recall
Platonic converse. Let the screech-owl keep
Watch where the fat maize crowds the forest wall.
High by the talking waters grows the cane;
Wild by the salt-lick herds the forest game.

And let the graybeard say when men and maids
Come for his blessing: "This I leave to you!
The Indian dream came on me in these glades,
And some strange bird-or-beast word named me new.
Peace be to all who keep the wilderness.
Cursed be the child who lets the freehold pass."

LINES WRITTEN FOR ALLEN TATE
ON HIS SIXTIETH ANNIVERSARY

The sound of guns from beleaguered Donelson
Up-river flowed again to Benfolly's hearth.
Year to familiar year we had heard it run
World-round and back, till Lytle cried out: "Earth
Is good, but better is land, and best
A land still fought-for, even in retreat;
For how else can Aeneas find his rest
And the child hearken and dream at his grandsire's feet?"

You said: "Not Troy is falling now. Time falls
And the victor locks himself in his victory
Deeming by that conceit he cancels walls
To step with Descartes and Comte beyond history.
But that kildee's cry is more than phylon or image
For us, deliberate exiles, whose dry rod
Blossoms athwart the Long Street's servile rage
And tells what pilgrimage greens the Tennessee sod."

So, Allen, you have kindled many an evening
When the creed of memory summoned us to your fire.
I remember that blazon, remember the firelight blessing
Owsley's uplifted head, Ransom's gray eye,
The Kentucky voice of Warren, until that household's
Oaken being spoke like a plucked lyre
And we turned as men who see where a battle unfolds;

And as now, once more, I see young faces turn
Where the battle is and a lonelier kildee's cry,
Exultant with your verses to unlearn
The bondage of their dead times' sophistry;
They know, by Mississippi, Thames, or Seine,
What city we build, what land we dream to save,
What art and wisdom are the part of men
And are your music, gallant and grave.

Among these—if with shortened breath—I come
Bearing an old friend's garland in these lines,
Scarred but surviving the Telchins' lance and bomb
To join the long procession where it winds
Up to a mountain home—
No marshals but the Muses for this day
Who in other years did not veil their sacred glance
Or from you look askance
And will not cast you off when you are gray.

REFUGEES

And if men ask you why you fled, and what,
Will you make answer, then? The age is not
Friendly to riddling, wants its discourse plain.
Its microphone, geared to the leaping clocks,
Tells all, loud-speaking, what will wax or wane,
Immediate and conclusive; flashes out
The dog's fanged answer to the dragging fox.
Will have its blood. Knows what it is about.

And this is riddling—or a cricket's cry.

It was red morning when the young men came
And saw, girdled with enemies, the flame
Swallowing the wreck where some had chosen to die.
Unrecognized, unknown, their weapons hid,
They sauntered there, unbid,
And in the desolate glare while stones cried out
Swore blood-feud from that day.
And now, a hardy few, in rocky ground,
Untaken and unwanted still they range.

From *Bread Loaf Anthology*. Edited by W. Storrs Lee. Preface by Robert Frost.
Middlebury College Press, Middlebury, Vermont, 1939.

Alec Brock Stevenson

HE WHO LOVED BEAUTY

"I have not seen one who loves virtue as he loves beauty."
—*Confucius.*

Dolorous, here he made his stand
Like those who are beaten,
Behind, the mountains, and in front, the sea,
To the west a rock by the brown river eaten.
Here beauty went along the strand
Smashing green waves against the white sand.

"Beyond the rock there, that's his thatch."
So spoke up a neighbor.
"And you'll be finding leather string on latch
And him inside, at peace from labor."

So he was run in, the fox to his earth,
He the old reaver, warm by his hearth,
But where was the booty, the gems and doubloons
Filched from fat merchants by tropical moons?
He, of all pirates prime hierophant,
No swords, no silver, no silk of Levant?
"Four things," he answered, "of all things that are:

A rock, a river, a tree and a star!"
This is his wisdom? He welcomed me ill;
I passed by the tree and strove up the hill.
This is the saying of one wise as he?
A river, a rock, a star and a tree?

This is the place, the shrine of the sage,
Who lived his last days with beauty for wage.
Here's where the tree was long ago humbled,
And a space points us out where granite has crumbled.
The river is empty, and a wind sweeps the stones;
The stars are not whiter than freebooter's bones.

SONNET

If it be night then, when the screech-owl's call
Divides at once the moon's beam and the oak;
If it be night, then, and not noon, the stroke
May from the ruined bell not last of all
Disjoin the time.
               There will be wind at night
And stars. Small cries of disembodied birds,
Remembered echoes of forgotten words
Your lips have framed, will linger, and no light
Come to discover whether There or Here
I see the dwarf blue iris in the stones,
Or when, with a quick terror in the bones,
Dismembered constellations float too near
And my two eyes, concise as lightning, seize
The dense geometry of Pleiades.

DEATH, MY COMPANION*

Death, my companion, who shall quit me soon
But not too soon, between the dusk and dawn,
The first to take my hand, the latest gone,
Must eat my bread at morning night and noon
And drink my drink and lie here on my bed,
Too far for speech but breathing all my breath
And thinking what a lonely man is Death.
But when, the last crust gnawed, the last word said,
You stand on these, I on the other shores,
I'll be the lonelier then, I think, to see
You so disdainful of eternity,
How soon you open the expectant doors
To clink your cup once more with dying men,
And you not caring to be born again.

* This poem and the succeeding poem are published here for the first time.

A HEMLOCK AT SUNSET

No poisoned image yours against the sky:
Not yours the hemlock which the wisest Greek
As who should death but as a surcease seek
Imbibed in studied willingness to die.
Through you the swallows play and breezes sigh,
And past your feathered boughs with homeward beak
The herons labor. From your topmost peak
Floats restless down a hawk's sad keening cry.

Ah, gently stirring silhouette of life,
And frail as painted on an Orient fan,
That glory glowing through your tattered grace
In fervid red and burnished gold, is rife
With stormy shock and clash, not other than
Thy hates and triumphs flashing through thy face.

ICARUS IN NOVEMBER

Icare est chut ici, le jeune audacieux.
                    —Philippe Desportes (1546-1606)

There is a moment blind with light, split by the hum
    Of something struck and shaken otherwhere,
And if breath's pausing stills the heartbeat and the dumb
    Wet trees clutch each last leaf, then on the air
Will blow, slow, small and keen, and faster greater higher,
    The hissing whoop of wind through timeless wings,
A thuttering drumbeat round a cold immortal fire
    Half muffling such a cruel cry as brings
    Fear to the lonely soul's imaginings—
A crescent wailing, and the little heart inclined
Hears Icarus, and how the chill gale moans behind.

What said, O Sun, to Icarus that he must fly
    Or fall, who dropped on this green wave at last?
Who fed him bitter aether from the tenuous sky,
    Whirled in his winged mind all that is past
And pointed four directions to his stumbling soul,
    Quibbled the whence how where when who and what
Till golden antlers blossomed and the Tree was whole
    And Dian poised, and Icarus forgot
    What Icarus had been and what had not,
And searching lost the hope that Icarus designed
And, seeing, never saw that Icarus was blind?

O Icarus is fallen, alabaster foam
    Hangs stilly, still, *Icare est chut ici.*
White tangent to the green wave's arc he's shotten home
    Man-bird, sky-arrow to the unriddling sea,
Who was so questing, still unsated, lost to act,
    Quartered the zig-zag sky for beauty's use,
Swooped, soared, sailed, wheeled, and turned and sudden
        stooped on fact

Or use's beauty, or the keen mind's loose
Hot ions streaming in a fluent sluice,
Heedless that Icarus must fall against the wind,
Echoing, ever falling in the hollow mind.
Sun of my night, lamp of my not uncertain void,
    Here Icarus is fallen, here he lies.
O fallen Icarus, whose fleshly eyes alloyed
    The fire and solar gold and still are eyes,
Give me some manner back the brain, the hardiness!
    If Icarus is fallen, once he flew:
Hard-taloned on the sunward wrist he scorned the jess,
    Pressed on his quarry in aethereal blue.
    Icare est chut ici, and still he knew
Less where the heron went than what he hoped to find,
And more the cloven hoofprint than the frightened hind.

Sidney Mttron Hirsch

QUODLIBET
TO J. H. F.

To walk in quiet lanes and fields—
To laugh in tune with brooks,
To learn how womanly the earth
In secret shadowed nooks
Is guarded from herself and streams
By strong-ribbed manlike rocks—
To move—to dream my dreams—
These things I love so deep
No fear have I of when I'll rest
Where promised flowers sleep;
Though now in mystic necromancy
Gain I but fitful gleams
The phantoms of my days shall be
The creatures of my dream.

To walk down quiet lanes in books,
To see the Men-gods there;
To bear their tranquil, valiant looks,
To breathe that mystic air;
To view their lives majestical
And courage debonair:
These things I love so deep

That I am stolen from myself
This royal tryst to keep.
And though I go there to and fro
As child to friendly dark,
A mild and stately seneschal
Admits me to the park.
Slow down the Gothic wooded lanes
I search with timid mien,
Until an awesome prophet deigns
To pace the sylvan scene.
With modest eye and furtive glance
I drink that blessed Grail
And win the Secret of the Lance,
And knight in nigril mail.
But yet another prize I win,
The Sage lifts noble eye
Not disapprovingly on me—
The child against the sky;
The Prince who walked amongst the stars
He stooped to look at me.
I hide this jewel in a joy
That wife will never see;
A treasure for a withered age,
Strange crystal for like's night,
A pinion that defeats the cage,
My thorn and crownless plight.
Yet in the moon of memory
These things I love so deep
No fear have I of when I'll rest
Where withered youth's asleep.

Allen Tate

TO INTELLECTUAL DETACHMENT

This is the man who classified the bits
Of his friends' hells into a pigeonhole—
He hung each disparate anguish on the spits
Parboiled and roasted in his own withering soul.

God give him peace! He gave none other peace.
His conversation glided on the brain
Like a razor honing in promise of one's decease—
Smooth like cold steel, yet feeling without pain;

And as his art, disjected from his mind,
Was utterly a tool, so it possessed him;
A passionate devil, informed in humankind,
It turned on him—he's dead. Shall we detest him?

NON OMNIS MORIAR

I ask you: Has the Singer sung
    The drear quintessence of the Song?
John Ford knew more than I of death,
    John Ford to death has passed along.

I ask you: Has the Singer said
    Wherefore his greatness is not dust?
Marlowe went muttering to death
    When he had done with song and lust.

And so I speak no other word,
    Nor ask where go the jaunty throng,
For laughter frames the lips of death—
    Death frames the Singer and the Song.

DEATH OF LITTLE BOYS

When little boys grown patient at last, weary,
Surrender their eyes immeasurably to the night,
The event will rage terrific as the sea;
Their bodies fill a crumbling room with light.

Then you will touch at the bedside, torn in two,
Gold curls now deftly intricate with gray
As the windowpane extends a fear to you
From one peeled aster drenched with the wind all day.

And over his chest the covers in the ultimate dream
Will mount to the teeth, ascend the eyes, press back
The locks—while round his sturdy belly gleam
Suspended breaths, white spars above the wreck:

Till all the guests, come in to look, turn down
Their palms, and delirium assails the cliff
Of Norway where you ponder, and your little town
Reels like a sailor drunk in a rotten skiff.

The bleak sunshine shrieks its chipped music then
Out to the milkweed amid the fields of wheat.
There is a calm for you where men and women
Unroll the chill precision of moving feet.

THE MEDITERRANEAN

Quem das finem, rex magne, dolorum?

Where we went in the boat was a long bay
A slingshot wide, walled in by towering stone—
Peaked margin of antiquity's delay,
And we went there out of time's monotone:

Where we went in the black hull no light moved
But a gull white-winged along the feckless wave,
The breeze, unseen but fierce as a body loved,
That boat drove onward like a willing slave:

Where we went in the small ship the seaweed
Parted and gave to us the murmuring shore,
And we made feast and in our secret need
Devoured the very plates Aeneas bore:

Where derelict you see through the low twilight
The green coast that you, thunder-tossed, would win,
Drop sail, and hastening to drink all night
Eat dish and bowl to take that sweet land in!

Where we feasted and caroused on the sandless
Pebbles, affecting our day of piracy,
What prophecy of eaten plates could landless
Wanderers fulfil by the ancient sea?

We for that time might taste the famous age
Eternal here yet hidden from our eyes
When lust of power undid its stuffless rage;
They, in a wineskin, bore earth's paradise.

Let us lie down once more by the breathing side
Of Ocean, where our live forefathers sleep
As if the Known Sea still were a month wide—
Atlantis howls but is no longer steep!

What country shall we conquer, what fair land
Unman our conquest and locate our blood?
We've cracked the hemispheres with careless hand!
Now, from the Gates of Hercules we flood

Westward, westward till the barbarous brine
Whelms us to the tired land where tasseling corn,
Fat beans, grapes sweeter than muscadine
Rot on the vine: in that land were we born.

AENEAS AT WASHINGTON

I myself saw furious with blood
Neoptolemus, at his side the black Atridae,
Hecuba and the hundred daughters, Priam
Cut down, his filth drenching the holy fires.
In that extremity I bore me well,
A true gentleman, valorous in arms,
Disinterested and honourable. Then fled:
That was a time when civilization
Run by the few fell to the many, and
Crashed to the shout of men, the clang of arms:
Cold victualing I seized, I hoisted up
The old man my father upon my back,
In the smoke made by sea for a new world
Saving little—a mind imperishable
If time is, a love of past things tenuous
As the hesitation of receding love.

(To the reduction of uncitied littorals
We brought chiefly the vigor of prophecy,
Our hunger breeding calculation
And fixed triumphs)

                          I saw the thirsty dove
In the glowing fields of Troy, hemp ripening
And tawny corn, the thickening Blue Grass
All lying rich forever in the green sun.
I see all things apart, the towers that men
Contrive I too contrived long, long ago.
Now I demand little. The singular passion
Abides its object and consumes desire
In the circling shadow of its appetite.
There was a time when the young eyes were slow,
Their flame steady beyond the firstling fire,
I stood in the rain, far from home at nightfall
By the Potomac, the great Dome lit the water,

The city my blood had built I knew no more
While the screech-owl whistled his new delight
Consecutively dark.

                              Stuck in the wet mire
Four thousand leagues from the ninth buried city
I thought of Troy, what we had built her for.

ODE TO THE CONFEDERATE DEAD

Row after row with strict impunity
The headstones yield their names to the element,
The wind whirrs without recollection;
In the riven troughs the splayed leaves
Pile up, of nature the casual sacrament
To the seasonal eternity of death;
Then driven by the fierce scrutiny
Of heaven to their election in the vast breath,
They sough the rumour of mortality.

Autumn is desolation in the plot
Of a thousand acres where these memories grow
From the inexhaustible bodies that are not
Dead, but feed the grass row after rich row.
Think of the autumns that have come and gone!—
Ambitious November with the humors of the year,
With a particular zeal for every slab,
Staining the uncomfortable angels that rot
On the slabs, a wing chipped here, an arm there:
The brute curiosity of an angel's stare
Turns you, like them, to stone,
Transforms the heaving air
Till plunged to a heavier world below
You shift your sea-space blindly
Heaving, turning like the blind crab.

Dazed by the wind, only the wind
The leaves flying, plunge

You know who have waited by the wall
The twilight certainty of an animal,
Those midnight restitutions of the blood
You know—the immitigable pines, the smoky frieze
Of the sky, the sudden call: you know the rage,
The cold pool left by the mounting flood,
Of muted Zeno and Parmenides.
You who have waited for the angry resolution

Of those desires that should be yours tomorrow,
You know the unimportant shrift of death
And praise the vision
And praise the arrogant circumstance
Of those who fall
Rank upon rank, hurried beyond decision—
Here by the sagging gate, stopped by the wall.

   Seeing, seeing only the leaves
   Flying, plunge and expire

Turn your eyes to the immoderate past,
Turn to the inscrutable infantry rising
Demons out of the earth—they will not last.
Stonewall, Stonewall, and the sunken fields of hemp.
Shiloh, Antietam, Malvern Hill, Bull Run.
Lost in that orient of the thick-and-fast
You will curse the setting sun.

   Cursing only the leaves crying
   Like an old man in a storm

You hear the shout, the crazy hemlocks point
With troubled fingers to the silence which
Smothers you, a mummy, in time.

                   The hound bitch
Toothless and dying, in a musty cellar
Hears the wind only.

             Now that the salt of their blood
Stiffens the saltier oblivion of the sea,
Seals the malignant purity of the flood,
What shall we who count our days and bow
Our heads with a commemorial woe
In the ribboned coats of grim felicity,
What shall we say of the bones, unclean,
Whose verdurous anonymity will grow?
The ragged arms, the ragged heads and eyes

Lost in these acres of the insane green?
The gray lean spiders come, they come and go;
In a tangle of willows without light
The singular screech-owl's tight
Invisible lyric seeds the mind
With the furious murmur of their chivalry.

   We shall say only the leaves
   Flying, plunge and expire

We shall say only the leaves whispering
In the improbable mist of nightfall
That flies on multiple wing;
Night is the beginning and the end

And in between the ends of distraction
Waits mute speculation, the patient curse
That stones the eyes, or like the jaguar leaps
For his own image in a jungle pool, his victim.

What shall we say who have knowledge
Carried to the heart? Shall we take the act
To the grave? Shall we, more hopeful, set up the grave
In the house? The ravenous grave?

                     Leave now
The shut gate and the decomposing wall:
The gentle serpent, green in the mulberry bush,
Riots with his tongue through the hush—
Sentinel of the grave who counts us all!

MR. POPE

When Alexander Pope strolled in the city
Strict was the glint of pearl and gold sedans.
Ladies leaned out more out of fear than pity
For Pope's tight back was rather a goat's than man's.

Often one thinks the urn should have more bones
Than skeletons provide for speedy dust,
The urn gets hollow, cobwebs brittle as stones
Weave to the funeral shell a frivolous rust.

And he who dribbled couplets like a snake
Coiled to a lithe precision in the sun
Is missing. The jar is empty; you may break
It only to find that Mr. Pope is gone.

What requisitions of a verity
Prompted the wit and rage between his teeth
One cannot say. Around a crooked tree
A moral climbs whose name should be a wreath.

LAST DAYS OF ALICE

Alice grown lazy, mammoth but not fat,
Declines upon her lost and twilight age;
Above in the dozing leaves the grinning cat
Quivers forever with his abstract rage:

Whatever light swayed on the perilous gate
Forever sways, nor will the arching grass,
Caught when the world clattered, undulate
In the deep suspension of the looking-glass.

Bright Alice! always pondering to gloze
The spoiled cruelty she had meant to say
Gazes learnedly down her airy nose
At nothing, nothing thinking all the day.

Turned absent-minded by infinity
She cannot move unless her double move,
The All-Alice of the world's entity
Smashed in the anger of her hopeless love,

Love for herself who, as an earthly twain,
Pouted to join her two in a sweet one;
No more the second lips to kiss in vain
The first she broke, plunged through the glass alone—

Alone to the weight of impassivity,
Incest of spirit, theorem of desire,
Without will as chalky cliffs by the sea,
Empty as the bodiless flesh of fire:

All space, that heaven is a dayless night,
A nightless day driven by perfect lust
For vacancy, in which her bored eyesight
Stares at the drowsy cubes of human dust.

—We too back to the world shall never pass
Through the shattered door, a dumb shade-harried crowd
Being all infinite, function depth and mass
Without figure, a mathematical shroud

Hurled at the air—blesséd without sin!
O God of our flesh, return us to Your wrath,
Let us be evil could we enter in
Your grace, and falter on the stony path!

SEASONS OF THE SOUL
To the memory of John Peale Bishop, 1892-1944

Allor porsi la mano un poco avante,
e colsi un ramicel da un gran pruno;
e il tronco suo gridò: Perchè mi schiante?

I. SUMMER

Summer, this is our flesh,
The body you let mature;
If now while the body is fresh
You take it, shall we give
The heart, lest heart endure
The mind's tattering
Blow of greedy claws?
Shall mind itself still live
If like a hunting king
It falls to the lion's jaws?

Under the summer's blast
The soul cannot endure
Unless by sleight or fast
It seize or deny its day
To make the eye secure.
Brothers-in-arms, remember
The hot wind dries and draws
With circular delay
The flesh, ash from the ember,
Into the summer's jaws.

It was a gentle sun
When, at the June solstice
Green France was overrun
With caterpillar feet.
No head knows where its rest is
Or may lie down with reason
When war's usurping claws
Shall take the heart escheat—

ALLEN TATE   73

Green field in burning season
To stain the weevil's jaws.
The southern summer dies
Evenly in the fall:
We raise our tired eyes
Into a sky of glass,
Blue, empty, and tall
Without tail or head
Where burn the equal laws
For Balaam and his ass
Above the invalid dead,
Who cannot lift their jaws.

When was it that the summer
(Daylong a liquid light)
And a child, the new-comer,
Bathed in the same green spray,
Could neither guess the night?
The summer had no reason;
Then, like a primal cause
It had its timeless day
Before it kept the season
Of time's engaging jaws.

Two men of our summer world
Descended winding hell
And when their shadows curled
They fearfully confounded
The vast concluding shell:
Stopping, they saw in the narrow
Light a centaur pause
And gaze, then his astounded
Beard, with a notched arrow,
Part back upon his jaws.

II. AUTUMN

It had an autumn smell
And that was how I knew
That I was down a well:

I was no longer young;
My lips were numb and blue,
The air was like fine sand
In a butcher's stall
Or pumice to the tongue:
And when I raised my hand
I stood in the empty hall.

The round ceiling was high
And the gray light like shale
Thin, crumbling, and dry:
No rug on the bare floor
Nor any carved detail
To which the eye could glide;
I counted along the wall
Door after closed door
Through which a shade might slide
To the cold and empty hall.

I will leave this house, I said,
There is the autumn weather—
Here, nor living nor dead;
The lights burn in the town
Where men fear together.
Then on the bare floor,
But tiptoe lest I fall,
I walked years down
Towards the front door
At the end of the empty hall.

The door was false—no key
Or lock, and I was caught
In the house; yet I could see
I had been born to it
For miles of running brought
Me back where I began.
I saw now in the wall
A door open a slit
And a fat grizzled man
Come out into the hall:

ALLEN TATE   75

As in a moonlit street
Men meeting are too shy
To check their hurried feet
But raise their eyes and squint
As through a needle's eye
Into the faceless gloom,—
My father in a gray shawl
Gave me an unseeing glint
And entered another room!
I stood in the empty hall

And watched them come and go
From one room to another,
Old men, old women—slow,
Familiar; girls, boys;
I saw my downcast mother
Clad in her street-clothes,
Her blue eyes long and small,
Who had no look or voice
For him whose vision froze
Him in the empty hall.

III. WINTER

Goddess sea-born and bright,
Return into the sea
Where eddying twilight
Gathers upon your people—
Cold goddess, hear our plea!
Leave the burnt earth, Venus,
For the drying God above,
Hanged in his windy steeple,
No longer bears for us
The living wound of love.

All the sea-gods are dead.
You, Venus, come home
To your salt maidenhead,
The tossed anonymous sea

Under shuddering foam—
Shade for lovers, where
A shark swift as your dove
Shall pace our company
All night to nudge and tear
The livid wound of love.

And now the winter sea:
Within her hollow rind
What sleek facility
Of sea-conceited scop
To plumb the nether mind!
Eternal winters blow
Shivering flakes, and shove
Bodies that wheel and drop—
Cold soot upon the snow
Their livid wound of love.

Beyond the undertow
The gray sea-foliage
Transpires a phosphor glow
Into the circular miles:
In the centre of his cage
The pacing animal
Surveys the jungle cove
And slicks his slithering wiles
To turn the venereal awl
In the livid wound of love.

Beyond the undertow
The rigid madrepore
Resists the winter's flow—
Headless, unageing oak
That gives the leaf no more.
Wilfully as I stood
Within the thickest grove
I seized a branch, which broke;
I heard the speaking blood
(From the livid wound of love)

Drip down upon my toe:
"We are the men who died
Of self-inflicted woe,
Lovers whose stratagem
Led to their suicide."
I touched my sanguine hair
And felt it drip above
Their brother who, like them,
Was maimed and did not bear
The living wound of love.

IV. SPRING

Irritable spring, infuse
Into the burning breast
Your combustible juice
That as a liquid soul
Shall be the body's guest
Who lights, but cannot stay
To comfort this unease
Which, like a dying coal,
Hastens the cooler day
Of the mother of silences.

Back in my native prime
I saw the orient corn
All space but no time,
Reaching for the sun
Of the land where I was born:
It was a pleasant land
Where even death could please
Us with an ancient pun—
All dying for the hand
Of the mother of silences.

In time of bloody war
Who will know the time?
Is it a new spring star
Within the timing chill,
Talking, or just a mime,

That rises in the blood—
Thin Jack-and Jilling seas
Without the human will?
Its light is at the flood,
Mother of silences!

It burns us each alone
Whose burning arrogance
Burns up the rolling stone,
This earth—Platonic cave
Of vertiginous chance!
Come, tired Sisyphus,
Cover the cave's egress
Where light reveals the slave,
Who rests when sleeps with us
The mother of silences.

Come, old woman, save
Your sons who have gone down
Into the burning cave:
Come, mother, and lean
At the window with your son
And gaze through its light frame
These fifteen centuries
Upon the shirking scene
Where men, blind, go lame:
Then, mother of silences,

Speak, that we may hear;
Listen, while we confess
That we conceal our fear;
Regard us, while the eye
Discerns by sight or guess
Whether, as sheep foregather
Upon their crooked knees,
We have begun to die;
Whether your kindness, mother,
Is mother of silences.

THE SWIMMERS

SCENE: *Montgomery County, Kentucky, July 1911*

Kentucky water, clear springs: a boy fleeing
   To water under the dry Kentucky sun,
   His four little friends in tandem with him, seeing

Long shadows of grapevine wriggle and run
   Over the green swirl; mullein under the ear
   Soft as Nausicaä's palm; sullen fun

Savage as childhood's thin harmonious tear:
   O fountain, bosom source undying-dead
   Replenish me the spring of love and fear

And give me back the eye that looked and fled
   When a thrush idling in the tulip tree
   Unwound the cold dream of the copperhead.

—Along the creek the road was winding; we
   Felt the quicksilver sky. I see again
   The shrill companions of that odyssey:

Bill Eaton, Charlie Watson, "Nigger" Layne
   The doctor's son, Harry Duèsler who played
   The flute; and Tate, with water on the brain.

Dog-days: the dusty leaves where rain delayed
   Hung low on poison-oak and scuppernong,
   And we were following the active shade

Of water, that bells and bickers all night long.
   "No more'n a mile," Layne said. All five stood still.
   Listening, I heard what seemed at first a song;

Peering, I heard the hooves come down the hill.
   The posse passed, twelve horse; the leader's face
   Was worn as limestone on an ancient sill.

Then, as sleepwalkers shift from a hard place
  In bed, and rising to keep a formal pledge
  Descend a ladder into empty space,

We scuttled down the bank below a ledge
  And marched stiff-legged in our common fright
  Along a hog-track by the riffle's edge:

Into a world where sound shaded the sight
  Dropped the dull hooves again; the horsemen came
  Again, all but the leader. It was night

Momently and I feared: eleven same
  Jesus-Christers unmembered and unmade,
  Whose Corpse had died again in dirty shame.

The bank then levelling in a speckled glade,
  We stopped to breathe above the swimming-hole;
  I gazed at its reticulated shade

Recoiling in blue fear, and felt it roll
  Over my ears and eyes and lift my hair
  Like seaweed tossing on a sunk atoll.

I rose again. Borne on the copper air
  A distant voice green as a funeral wreath
  Against a grave: "That dead nigger there."

The melancholy sheriff slouched beneath
  A giant sycamore; shaking his head
  He plucked a sassafras twig and picked his teeth:

"We come too late." He spoke to the tired dead
  Whose ragged shirt soaked up the viscous flow
  Of blood in which It lay discomfited.

A butting horse-fly gave one ear a blow
  And glanced off, as the sheriff kicked the rope
  Loose from the neck and hooked it with his toe

Away from the blood.—I looked back down the slope:
  The friends were gone that I had hoped to greet.—
  A single horseman came at a slow lope

And pulled up at the hanged man's horny feet;
  The sheriff noosed the feet, the other end
  The stranger tied to his pommel in a neat

Slip-knot. I saw the Negro's body bend
  And straighten, as a fish-line cast transverse
  Yields to the current that it must subtend.

The sheriff's Goddamn was a murmured curse
  Not for the dead but for the blinding dust
  That boxed the cortège in a cloudy hearse

And dragged it towards our town. I knew I must
  Not stay till twilight in that silent road;
  Sliding my bare feet into the warm crust,

I hopped the stonecrop like a panting toad
  Mouth open, following the heaving cloud
  That floated to the court-house square its load

Of limber corpse that took the sun for shroud.
  There were three figures in the dying sun
  Whose light were company where three was crowd.

My breath crackled the dead air like a shotgun
  As, sheriff and the stranger disappearing,
  The faceless head lay still. I could not run

Or walk, but stood. Alone in the public clearing
  This private thing was owned by all the town,
  Though never claimed by us within my hearing.

Merrill Moore

CUMAE

Gather noble death
And pour it on our land.
Make the wooden walls
Well manned.

With the ripe grain
Fill the earthen pots.
Gather all the grapes
And apricots.

Drive in the coarse swine
And kill the fat young beeves.
Scatter sweet spices
And bay leaves.

Bring white fleeces
And cloths of purple
To lay at the feet
Of the Sybil.

THE NOISE THAT TIME MAKES

The noise Time makes in passing by
Is very slight but even you can hear it
Having not necessarily to be near it,
Needing only the slightest will to try:
Hold the receiver of a telephone
To your ear when no one is talking on the line
And what may at first sound to you like the whine
Of wind over distant wires is Time's own

Garments brushing against a windy cloud.
That same noise again but not so well
Can be heard by taking a small cockle shell
From the sand and holding it against your head;
Then you can hear Time's footsteps as they pass
Over the earth brushing the eternal grass.

THE BOOK OF HOW

After the stars were all hung separately out
For mortal eyes to see that care to look
The One who did it sat down and wrote a book
On how He did it. It took Him about
As long to write the book as to do the deed,
But He said, "It's things like this we mostly need."
And the angels approved but the devils screamed with laughter
For they knew exactly what would follow after.

For somehow He managed entirely to omit
The most important facts in accomplishing it,
Where He got the ladder to reach the stars
And how he lighted them, especially Mars,
And what he hung them on when he got them there
Eternally distant, luminous in the air.

LITERATURE: THE GOD, ITS RITUAL

Something strange I do not comprehend
Is this: I start to write a certain verse
But by the time that I come to its end
Another has been written that is worse
Or possibly better than the one I meant,
And certainly not the same, and different.

I cannot understand it—I begin
A poem and then it changes as I write,
Never have I written the one I thought I might,
Never gone out the door that I came in,
Until I am perplexed by this perverse
Manner and behavior of my verse.

I've never written the poem that I intended;
The poem was always different when it ended.

Jesse Wills

TO A TIRED CLERK

Do not despair, though you are clipped with chains
Of petty drudging, clangor and grime will heal.
In loneliness your city's bones of steel
Will rust, green-tendoned; only the cool rains
Will whisper down old thunder-roads of trains;
And centuries long as today Nineveh counts
Will fret the marbles of old soda-founts
With sands which now are hotel window-panes.

It yet may be, when glittering frost has thinned
The leaves that hide, by westering yellow fires
Nomads, bronze-armed, shall note where mystery carves
Your firm's worn name, and dread their wizard sires,
Curbing their foam-necked horses, while their scarves
And ruddy hair are strung upon the wind.

THE WATCHERS

Beneath the super market's neon glow,
The goods high piled, the hands, the scuffling feet;
Beneath the asphalt of the outside street,
The parking cars; stone coffined in a row,
Holding their tools, an arrow point, a hoe,
The dead sleep by their pots of figured clay.
The hills beyond, our link with yesterday.
That watch us now, once saw these long ago,

Dark in the twilight, green in varied Spring,
In Autumn's war paint—soil too thin to plow—
Hills that recall the tom-toms whispering,
You lifted up your feather crest of trees.
Changeless above mound builder mysteries.
What will you see five centuries from now?

HALF SAID

I've lived in half-way houses all my life,
Known nature half-way, half-way shared the art
Of blending flowers, or words; with half a heart
Have served my business; through religious strife
Kept half-way faith; without the drum and fife
Of certitude and triumph, or the smart
Of abject failure, played a paper part
With half-known facts with which my mind is rife.

Beyond the hills the serried mountains rise.
Some venture part-way up, admire the view,
Then take the safe path down; a stubborn few
Strive to the final peak in frozen skies;
But others linger half-way, envying those
Who top the roaring gulfs the eagle knows.

THE FUGITIVES

They cannot here their youth renew.
Reversing years, again review
Old meetings and the plans they drew.

These yellowed pages, scraps of rime,
Detritus of a far gone time,
What once was live, can only mime.

If one seeks sources, verity
Is here, mementoes, history,
But still remains the mystery

Of how and why in those few years
Unequals formed a group of peers
And from brief verse built fame, careers.

No cairn, this is a dwelling place
For script or printed words that trace
Evolvement of an inner grace.

These halls that proper honors give,
Maintaining forms, are like a sieve;
The spirit still is fugitive.

Laura Riding

DIMENSIONS

Measure me for a burial
That my low stone may neatly say
In a precise, Euclidean way
How I am three-dimensional.

Yet can life be so thin and small?
Measure me in time. But time is strange
And still and knows no rule or change
But death and death is nothing at all.

Measure me by beauty.
But beauty is death's earliest name
For life, and life's first dying, a flame
That glimmers, an amaranth that will fade
And fade again in death's dim shade.

Measure me not by beauty, that fears strife.
For beauty makes peace with death, buying
Dishonor and eternal dying
That she may keep outliving life.

Measure me then by love—yet, no,
For I remember times when she
Sought her own measurements in me,
But fled, afraid I might foreshow
How broad I was myself and tall
And deep and many-measured, moving
My scale upon her and thus proving
That both of us were nothing at all.

Measure me by myself
And not by time or love or space
Or beauty. Give me this last grace:
That I may be on my low stone
A gage unto myself alone.
I would not have these old faiths fall
To prove that I was nothing at all.

SUMMARY FOR ALASTOR

Because my song was bold
And you knew but my song,
You thought it must belong
To one brave to behold.

But finding me a shy
And cool and quiet Eve,
You scarcely would believe
The fevered singer was I.

And you caressed the child
That blushed beneath your eyes,
Hoping you might surprise
The hidden heart and wild.

And being only human,
A proud, impetuous fool
Whose guise alone was cool,
I let you see the woman.

Yet, though I was beguiled
Through being all too human,
I'm glad you had the woman
And not the trustful child.

For though the woman's weeping
And still must weep awhile,
The dreaming child can smile
And keep on safely sleeping.

VIRGIN OF THE HILLS

My flesh is at a distance from me.
Yet approach and touch it:
It is as near as anyone can come.

Already this vestiary stuff
Is all that's left of me,
Though I have never worn it,
Though I shall never be dead.

Accept the premature relic.
Such acts are irredeemable,
Perversely immortal,
Eternally unregrettable.

And I?
Meanwhile I recline remotely on these hills.
The mists thread apart, are retwisted by the wind.
There is a graveless peace
Neither dawn, neither death.

And the possession?
The violence will be over
And an old passion,
Before I leave these ancient hills,
Descend abruptly into the modern city, crying:
Love!

THE POET'S CORNER

Here where the end of bone is no end of song
And the earth is bedecked with immortality
In what was poetry
And now is pride beside
And nationality,
Here is a battle with no bravery
But if the coward's tongue has gone
Swording his own lusty lung.
Listen if here is victory
Written into a library
Waving the books in banners
Soldierly at last, for the lines
Go marching on, delivered of the soul.

And happily may they rest beyond
Suspicion now, the incomprehensibles
Traitorous in such talking
As chattered over their countries' boundaries.
The graves are gardened and the whispering
Stops at the hedges, there is singing
Of it in the ranks, there is a hush
Where the ground has limits
And the rest is loveliness.

And loveliness?
Death has an understanding of it
Loyal to many flags
And is a silent ally of any country
Beset in its mortal heart
With immortal poetry.

STARVED

Who owns this body of mine?
Not him to whom I gave it for a moment
To test the longing limit of his flesh upon,
Nor yet myself, its guardian.

Who owns this body of mine,
Come, take it back.
I have not fare enough for both of us.

Who owns this body of mine?
Will no one claim it?
I cannot bear to leave it so.
Pity me,
Pity the orphan frame,
Hungering together—
Death is the final crust
Of our poor provender.

THE ONLY DAUGHTER

Under her gown the girl is
And alone as any lonely daughter.
She is kept in green because
Green silk is nearly water

And removes her as she is nearly white.
Mother slept through her birth.
Father was with the coals that night
At a study of sparks by the hearth.

It was forgotten she came naked.
In the morning she was put in wool.
Her face left bare but blended
With the house out the window cool.

She has grown and has been given
Day by day unknown and dressed
The quiet mysteries of woman
Unwitting of the rhapsodist.

But it is dangerous to keep an only daughter
Like Atlantis or an isle
Sunken in green water
Through which may rise a smile.

She smiles and she is golden
About her mouth waving.
Her smile only will be stolen
And the mouth not worth saving

Will spread smooth and green
Over no more hunger.
How warm is chill if seen
When the body is yet younger

Than a green gown and the gown
Ripples like a summer winter
As the lotus-lilies drown
Of an only daughter.

Robert Graves

A VALENTINE

The hunter to the husbandman
Pays tribute since our love began,
And to love-loyalty dedicates
The phantom kills he meditates.
Let me embrace, embracing you,
Beauty of other shape and hue,
Odd glinting graces of which none
Shone more than candle to your sun;
Your well-kissed hand was beckoning me
In unfamiliar imagery.
Smile your forgiveness: each bright ghost
Dives in love's glory and is lost
Yielding your comprehensive pride
A homage, even to suicide.

John Gould Fletcher

THE LAST FRONTIER

Having passed over the world,
And seen three seas and two mountains,
He came to the last frontier.

On a hilltop
There were two men making a hole in the earth,
And beside it, his own dead body lay.

The thin man tugged at his beard
And wondered if the grave was deep enough,
The fat man sweated and toiled
And longed for a glass of beer.

Meanwhile his body lay there,
In a shabby suit, on its bed of wet earth;
And the clouds of evening, blown from beyond the world,
Swung lightly over his face.

But he waited until
His old body was dropped and the earth shovelled deeply upon
   it,
And the lean man put up a cross,
While the fat man stumped away home.

Then he went back from the last frontier
To the countries he had known years ago;
To the seven hotels and the thirty-two deserts
Without hope.

Hart Crane

STARK MAJOR

The lover's death, how regular
With lifting spring and starker
Vestiges of the sun, that somehow
Filter in to us before we waken.

Not yet is there that heat and sober
Vivisection of more clamant air
That hands joined in the dark will answer
After the daily circuits of its glare.

It is the time of sundering . . .
Beneath the green silk counterpane
Her mound of undelivered life
Lies cool upon her—not yet pain.

And she will wake before you pass,
Scarcely aloud, beyond her door,
And every third step down the stair
Until you reach the muffled floor—

Will laugh and call your name; while you,
Still answering her faint good-byes,
Will find the street, only to look
At doors and stone with broken eyes.

Walk now, and note the lover's death.
Henceforth her memory is more
Than yours, in cries, in ecstasies
You cannot ever reach to share.

Andrew Nelson Lytle

EDWARD GRAVES

Here where the honey-suckle vines grow wan,
Besieged by bugs that suck their green leaves yellow,
Well darned in sixty-odd winters' rusts and lines,
Sits old Graves on his porch all kinds of weather,
And ponders with his outside eyes turned in,
While mongrel hens seek out with lowered beaks
The bugs, well-filled with honey blood and bloom.

The browning honey-horns droop and faint,
Exhale in rainbow drops a timorous essence,
And spend their whiff of fragrance all unheeded
On lustful winds who whirl far to the South,
Heated with expectation of lying that night
On the voluptuous breast of weeping willow,
Flowing its hair beside some moon-lit river.

It hasn't always been like this with Edward Graves!—
He used to climb the top of Pilot's Knob
To see fresh color poured in the morning sky,
Or watch at eve the sparks fly out and hit the dusk
As the Master Mechanic ground the sun between
The flinty sides of distant jagged hills
To shine and clean it for the coming day.

What changed him so?
One evening he came to supper a trifle late,
And found the meat still frying on the stove,
The table set, and Jane run off with a show.

Robert Penn Warren

TO A FACE IN A CROWD

Brother, my brother, whither do you pass?
Unto what hill at dawn, unto what glen,
Where among the rocks the faint lascivious grass
Fingers in lust the arrogant bones of men?

Beside what bitter waters will you go
Where the lean gulls of your heart along the shore
Rehearse to the cliffs the rhetoric of their woe?
In dream, perhaps, I have seen your face before.

A certain night has borne both you and me;
We are the children of an ancient band
Broken between the mountains and the sea.
A cromlech marks for you that utmost strand

And you must find the dolorous place they stood.
Of old I know that shore, that dim terrain,
And know how black and turbulent the blood
Will beat through iron chambers of the brain

When at your back the taciturn tall stone,
Which is your fathers' monument and mark,
Repeats the waves' implacable monotone,
Ascends the night and propagates the dark.

Men there have lived who wrestled with the ocean;
I was afraid—the polyp was their shroud.
I was afraid. That shore of your decision
Awaits beyond this street where in the crowd

Your face is blown, an apparition, past.
Renounce the night as I, and we must meet
As weary nomads in this desert at last,
Borne in the lost procession of these feet.

AUBADE FOR HOPE

Dawn: and foot on the cold stair treading or
Thump of wood on the unswept hearth-stone is
Comment on the margin of consciousness,
A dirty thumb-smear by the printed page.

Thumb-smear: nay, other, for the blessèd light
Acclaimèd thus, as a ducal progress by
The scared cur, wakes them that wallowed in
The unaimed faceless appetite of dream.

All night, the ice sought out the rotten bough:
In sleep they heard. And now they stir, as east
Beyond the formal gleam of landscape sun
Has struck the senatorial hooded hill.

Light; the groaning stair; the match aflame;
The Negro woman's hand, horned gray with cold,
That lit the wood—oh, merciless great eyes
Blank as the sea—I name some things that shall

As voices speaking from a farther room,
Muffled, bespeak us yet for time and hope:
For Hope that like a blockhead grandma ever
Above the ash and spittle croaks and leans.

CRIME

Envy the mad killer who lies in the ditch and grieves,
Hearing the horns on the highway, and the tires scream:
He tries to remember, and tries, but he cannot seem
To remember what it was he buried under the leaves.

By the steamed lagoon, near the carnivorous orchid,
Pirates hide treasure and mark the place with a skull,
Then lose the map, and roar in pubs with a skinful,
In Devon or Barbados; but remember what they hid.

But what was it? But he is too tired to ask it.
An old woman mumbling her gums like incertitude?
The proud stranger who asked the match by the park wood,
Or the child who crossed the park every day with the lunch-
            basket?

He cannot say, nor formulate the delicious
And smooth convolution of terror, like whipped cream,
Nor the mouth, rounded and white for the lyric scream
Which he never heard, though he still tries, nodding and
            serious.

His treasure: for years down streets of contempt and trouble
Hugged under his coat, among sharp elbows and rows
Of eyes hieratic like foetuses in jars;
Or he nursed it unwitting, like a child asleep with a bauble.

Happiness: what the heart wants. That is its fond
Definition, and wants only the peace in God's eye.
Our flame bends in that draft; and that is why
He clutched at the object bright on the bottom of the murky
            pond.

Peace, all he asked: past despair and past the uncouth
Violation, he snatched at the fleeting hem, though in error;
Nor gestured before the mind's sycophant mirror,
Nor made the refusal and spat from the secret side of his
        mouth.

Though a tree for you is a tree, and in the long
Dark, no sibilant tumor inside your enormous
Head, though no walls confer in the silent house,
Nor the eyes of pictures protrude, like snail's, each on its
        prong,

Yet envy him, for what he buried is buried
By the culvert there, till the boy with the air-gun
In spring, at the violet, comes; nor is ever known
To go on any vacations with him, lend money, break bread.

And envy him, for though the seasons stammer
Past pulse in the yellow throat of the field-lark,
Still memory drips, a pipe in the cellar-dark,
And in its hutch and hole, as when the earth gets warmer,

The cold heart heaves like a toad, and lifts its brow
With that bright jewel you have no use for now;
While puzzled yet, despised with the attic junk, the letter
Names over your name, and mourns under the dry rafter.

ORIGINAL SIN: A SHORT STORY

Nodding, its great head rattling like a gourd,
And locks like seaweed strung on the stinking stone,
The nightmare stumbles past, and you have heard
It fumble your door before it whimpers and is gone:
It acts like the old hound that used to snuffle your door and
moan.

You thought you had lost it when you left Omaha,
For it seemed connected then with your grandpa, who
Had a wen on his forehead and sat on the veranda
To finger the precious protuberance, as was his habit to do,
Which glinted in sun like rough garnet or the rich old brain
bulging through.

But you met it in Harvard Yard as the historic steeple
Was confirming the midnight with its hideous racket,
And you wondered how it had come, for it stood so imbecile,
With empty hands, humble, and surely nothing in pocket:
Riding the rods, perhaps—or grandpa's will paid the ticket.

You were almost kindly then, in your first homesickness,
As it tortured its stiff face to speak, but scarcely mewed;
Since then you have outlived all your homesickness,
But have met it in many another distempered latitude:
Oh, nothing is lost, ever lost! at last you understood.

But it never came in the quantum glare of sun
To shame you before your friends, and had nothing to do
With your public experience or private reformation:
But it thought no bed too narrow—it stood with lips askew
And shook its great head sadly like the abstract Jew.

ROBERT PENN WARREN   109

Never met you in the lyric arsenical meadows
When children call and your heart goes stone in the bosom;
At the orchard anguish never, nor ovoid horror,
Which is furred like a peach or avid like the delicious plum.
It takes no part in your classic prudence or fondled axiom.

Not there when you exclaimed: "Hope is betrayed by
Disastrous glory of sea-capes, sun-torment of whitecaps
—There must be a new innocence for us to be stayed by."
But there it stood, after all the timetables, all the maps,
In the crepuscular clutter of *always, always,* or *perhaps.*

You have moved often and rarely left an address,
And hear of the deaths of friends with a sly pleasure,
A sense of cleansing and hope, which blooms from distress;
But it has not died, it comes, its hand childish, unsure,
Clutching the bribe of chocolate or a toy you used to treasure.

It tries the lock; you hear, but simply drowse:
There is nothing remarkable in that sound at the door.
Later you may hear it wander the dark house
Like a mother who rises at night to seek a childhood picture;
Or it goes to the backyard and stands like an old horse cold in
        the pasture.

PURSUIT

The hunchback on the corner, with gum and shoelaces,
Has his own wisdom and pleasures, and may not be lured
To divulge them to you, for he has merely endured
Your appeal for his sympathy and your kind purchases;
And wears infirmity but as the general who turns
Apart, in his famous old greatcoat there on the hill
At dusk when the rapture and cannonade are still,
To muse withdrawn from the dead, from his gorgeous sub-
        alterns;
Or stares from the thicket of his familiar pain, like a fawn
That meets you a moment, wheels, in imperious innocence is
        gone.

Go to the clinic. Wait in the outer room
Where like an old possum the snag-nailed hand will hump
On its knee in murderous patience, and the pomp
Of pain swells like the Indies, or a plum.
And there you will stand, as on the Roman hill,
Stunned by each withdrawn gaze and severe shape,
The first barbarian victor stood to gape
At the sacrificial fathers, white-robed, still;
And even the feverish old Jew stares stern with authority
Till you feel like one who has come too late, or improperly
        clothed, to a party.

The doctor will take you now. He is burly and clean;
Listening, like lover or worshiper, bends at your heart;
But cannot make out just what it tries to impart;
So smiles; says you simply need a change of scene.
Of scene, of solace: therefore Florida,
Where Ponce de Leon clanked among the lilies,
Where white sails skit on blue and cavort like fillies,
And the shoulder gleams in the moonlit corridor.
A change of love: if love is a groping Godward, though blind,
No matter what crevice, cranny, chink, bright in dark, the pale
        tentacle find.

In Florida consider the flamingo
Its color passion but its neck a question;
Consider even that girl the other guests shun
On beach, at bar, in bed, for she may know
The secret you are seeking, after all;
Or the child you humbly sit by, excited and curly,
That screams on the shore at the sea's sunlit hurlyburly,
Till the mother calls its name, toward nightfall.
Till you sit alone: in the dire meridians, off Ireland, in fury
Of spume-tooth and dawnless sea-heave, salt rimes the
        lookout's devout eye.

Till you sit alone—which is the beginning of error—
Behind you the music and lights of the great hotel:
Solution, perhaps, is public, despair personal,
But history held to your breath clouds like a mirror.
There are many states, and towns in them, and faces,
But meanwhile, the little old lady in black, by the wall,
Who admires all the dancers, and tells you how just last fall
Her husband died in Ohio, and damp mists her glasses;
She blinks and croaks, like a toad or a Norn, in the horrible
        light,
And rattles her crutch, which may put forth a small bloom,
        perhaps white.

THE BALLAD OF BILLIE POTTS

(When I was a child I heard this story from an old lady who was a relative of mine. The scene, according to her version, was in the section of Western Kentucky known as "Between the Rivers," the region between the Cumberland and the Tennessee. Years later, I came across another version in a book on the history of the outlaws of the Cave Inn Rock, or the Cave-In-Rock. The name of Bardstown in the present account refers to Bardstown, Kentucky, where the first race track west of the mountains was laid out late in the Eighteenth Century.)

Big Billie Potts was big and stout
In the land between the rivers.
His shoulders were wide and his gut stuck out
Like a croker of nubbins and his holler and shout
Made the bob-cat shiver and the black-jack leaves shake
In the section between the rivers.
He would slap you on your back and laugh.

Big Billie had a wife, she was dark and little
In the land between the rivers,
And clever with her wheel and clever with her kettle,
But she never said a word and when she sat
By the fire her eyes worked slow and narrow like a cat
In the land between the rivers.
Nobody knew what was in her head.

They had a big boy with fuzz on his chin
So tall he ducked the door when he came in,
A clabber-headed bastard with snot in his nose
And big red wrists hanging out of his clothes
And a whicker when he laughed where his father had a beller
In the section between the rivers.
They called him Little Billie.
He was their darling.

(It is not hard to see the land, what it was.
Low hills and oak. The fetid bottoms where
The slough uncoiled and in the tangled cane,
Where no sun comes, the muskrat's astute face
Was lifted to the yammering jay; then dropped.
Some cabin where the shag-bark stood and the
Magnificent tulip-tree; both now are gone.
But the land is there, and as you top a rise,
Beyond you all the landscape steams and simmers
—The hills, now gutted, red, cane-brake and black-jack yet.
The oak leaf steams under the powerful sun.
"Mister, is this the right road to Paducah?"
The red face, seamed and gutted like the hill,
Slow under time, and with the innocent savagery
Of Time, the bleared eyes rolling, answers from
Your dream: "They names hit so, but I ain't bin.")

Big Billie was the kind who laughed but could spy
The place for a ferry where folks would come by.
He built an inn and folks bound West
Hitched their horses there to take their rest
And grease the gall and grease the belly
And jaw and spit under the trees
In the section between the rivers.

Big Billie said: "Git down, friend, and take yore ease!"
He would slap you on your back and set you at his table.

(Leaning and slow, you see them move
In massive passion colder than any love:
Their lips move but you do not hear the words
Nor trodden twig nor fluted irony of birds
Nor hear the rustle of the heart
That, heave and settle, gasp and start,
Heaves like a fish in the ribs' dark basket borne
West from the great water's depth whence it was torn.

Their names are like the leaves, but are forgot
—The slush and swill of the world's great pot

That foamed at the range's lip, and spilled
Like quicksilver across green baize, the unfulfilled
Disparate glitter, gleam, wild symptom, seed
Flung in the long wind: silent, proceed
Past meadow, salt-lick, and the lyric swale;
Enter the arbor, shadow of trees, fade, fail.)

Big Billie was sharp at swap and trade
And could smell the nest where the egg was laid,
He could read and cipher and they called him squire
In the land between the rivers.
And he added up his money while he sat by the fire
And sat in the shade while folks sweated and strove,
For he was the one who fatted and throve
In the section between the rivers.
"Thank you kindly, sir," Big Billie would say
When the man in the black coat paid him at streak of day
And swung to the saddle and was ready to go
And rode away and didn't know
That he was already as good as dead,
For at midnight the message had been sent ahead:
"Man in black coat, riding bay mare with star."

(There was a beginning but you cannot see it.
There will be an end but you cannot see it.
They will not turn their faces to you though you call,
Who pace a logic merciless as light,
Whose law is their long shadow on the grass,
Sun at the back; pace, pass,
And passing nod in that glacial delirium
While the tight sky shudders like a drum
And speculation rasps its idiot nails
Across the dry slate where you did the sum.

The answer is in the back of the book but the page is gone.
And grandma told you to tell the truth but she is dead.
And heedless, their hairy faces fixed
Beyond your call or question now, they move
Under the infatuate weight of their wisdom,

Precious but for the preciousness of their burden,
Sainted and sad and sage as the hairy ass, who bear
History like bound faggots, with stiff knees;
And breathe the immaculate climate where
The lucent leaf is lifted, lank beard fingered, by no breeze,
Rapt in the fabulous complacency of fresco, vase, or frieze:

And the testicles of the fathers hang down like old lace.)

Little Billie was full of piss and vinegar
And full of sap as a maple tree
And full of tricks as a lop-eared pup,
So one night when the runner didn't show up,
Big Billie called Little and said, "Saddle up,"
And nodded toward the man was taking his sup
With his belt unlatched and his feet to the fire.
Big Billie said, "Give Amos a try,
Fer this feller takes the South Fork and Amos'll be nigher
Than Baldy or Buster, and Amos is sly
And slick as a varmint, and I don't deny
I lak bizness with Amos fer he's one you kin trust
In the section between the rivers,
And hit looks lak they's mighty few.
Amos will split up fair and square."

Little Billie had something in his clabber-head
In addition to snot, and he reckoned he knew
How to skin a cat or add two and two.
So long before the sky got red
Over the land between the rivers,
He hobbled his horse back in the swamp
And squatted on his hams in the morning dew and damp
And scratched his stomach and grinned to think
How his Pap would be proud and his Mammy glad
To know what a thriving boy they had
In the section between the rivers.
He always was a good boy to his darling Mammy.

(Think of yourself riding away from the dawn,
Think of yourself and the unnamed ones who had gone
Before, riding, who rode away from *goodbye, goodbye,*
And toward *hello,* toward Time's unwinking eye;
And like the cicada had left, at cross-roads or square,
The old shell of self, thin, ghostly, translucent, light as air;
At dawn riding into the curtain of unwhispering green,
Away from the vigils and voices into the green
World, land of the innocent bough, land of the leaf.
Think of your face green in the submarine light of the leaf.

Or think of yourself crouched at the swamp-edge,
Dawn-silence past last owl-hoot and not yet at day-verge
First bird-stir, titmouse or drowsy warbler not yet.
You touch the grass in the dark and your hand is wet.
Then light: and you wait for the stranger's hoofs on the soft
        trace,
And under the green leaf's translucence the light bathes your
        face.

Think of yourself at dawn: Which are you? What?)

Little Billie heard hoofs on the soft grass,
But he squatted and let the rider pass,
For he didn't want to waste good lead and powder
Just to make the slough-fish and swamp-buzzards prouder
In the land between the rivers.
But he saw the feller's face and thanked his luck
It was the one Pap said was fit to pluck.
So he got on his horse and cantered up the trace.
Called, "Hi thar!" and the stranger watched him coming,
And sat his mare with a smile on his face,
Just watching Little Billie and smiling and humming
In the section between the rivers.
Little Billie rode up and the stranger said,
"Why, bless my heart, if it ain't Little Billie!"

"Good mornen," said Billie, and said, "My Pap
Found somethen you left and knowed you'd be missen,

And he ain't wanten nuthen not proper his'n."
But the stranger didn't do a thing but smile and listen
Polite as could be to what Billie said.
But he must have had eyes in the side of his head
As they rode along beside the slough
In the land between the rivers,
Or known what Billie was out to do,
For when Billie said, "Mister, I've brung hit to you,"
And reached his hand for it down in his britches,
The stranger just reached his own hand, too.

"Boom!" Billie's gun said, and the derringer, "Bang!"
"Oh, I'm shot!" Billie howled and grabbed his shoulder.
"Nor bad," said the stranger, "for you're born to hang,
But I'll save some rope 'fore you're a minute older
If you don't high-tail to your honest Pap
In the section between the rivers."
Oh, Billie didn't tarry and Billie didn't linger,
For Billie didn't trust the stranger's finger
And didn't admire the stranger's face
And didn't like the climate of the place,
So he turned and high-tailed up the trace,
With blood on his shirt and snot in his nose
And pee in his pants for he'd wet his clothes,
And the stranger just sits and admires how he goes,
And says, "Why, that boy would do right well back on the
        Bardstown track!"

"You fool!" said his Pap, but his Mammy cried
To see the place where the gore-blood dried
Round the little hole in her darling's hide.
She wiped his nose and patted his head,
But Pappy barred the door and Pappy said,
"That bastard has maybe got some friends
In the section between the rivers,
And you can't say how sich bizness ends
And a man ain't sure he kin trust his neighbors,
Fer thar's mortal spite fer him sweats and labors
Even here between the rivers."

He didn't ask Little how he felt,
But said, "Two hundred in gold's in my money belt,
And take the roan and the brand-new saddle
And stop yore blubberen and skeedaddle,
And the next time you try and pull a trick
Fer God's sake don't talk but do hit quick."
So Little Billie took his leave
And left his Mammy there to grieve
And left his Pappy in Old Kaintuck
And headed West to try his luck
And left the land between the rivers,
For it was Roll, Missouri,
It was Roll, roll, Missouri.

And he was gone nigh ten long year
And never sent word to give his Pappy cheer

Nor wet pen in ink for his Mammy dear.
For Little Billie never was much of a hand with a pen-staff.

(There is always another country and always another place.
There is always another name and another face.
And the name and the face are you, and you
The name and the face, and the stream you gaze into
Will show the adoring face, show the lips that lift to you
As you lean with the implacable thirst of self,
As you lean to the image which is yourself,
To set the lip to lip, fix eye on bulging eye,
To drink not of the stream but of your deep identity,
But water is water and it flows,
Under the image on the water the water coils and goes
And its own beginning and its end only the water knows.

There are many countries and the rivers in them
—Cumberland, Tennessee, Ohio, Colorado, Pecos, Little Big
      Horn,
And Roll, Missouri, roll.
But there is only water in them.

And in the new country and in the new place
The eyes of the new friend will reflect the new face
And his mouth will speak to frame
The syllables of the new name
And the name is you and is the agitation of the air
And is the wind and the wind runs and the wind is everywhere.

The name and the face are you.
The name and the face are always new
And they are you.
Are new.

For they have been dipped in the healing flood.
For they have been dipped in the redeeming blood.
For they have been dipped in Time
And Time is only beginnings
Time is only and always beginnings
And is the redemption of our crime
And is our Saviour's priceless blood.

For Time is always the new place,
And no-place.
For Time is always the new name and the new face,
And no-name and no-face.

For Time is motion
For Time is innocence
For Time is West.)

Oh, who is coming along the trace,
Whistling along in the late sunshine,
With a big black hat above his big red face
And a long black coat that swings so fine?
Oh, who is riding along the trace
Back to the land between the rivers,
With a big black beard growing down to his guts
And silver mountings on his pistol-butts
And a belt as broad as a saddle-girth
And a look in his eyes like he owned the earth?

And meets a man riding up the trace
And looks right sharp and scans his face
And says, "Durn if'n hit ain't Joe Drew!"
"I reckin hit's me," says Joe and gives a spit,
"But whupped if'n I figger how you knows hit,
Fer if'n I'm Joe, then who air you?"
And the man with the black beard says: "Why, I'm Little
    Billie!"
And Joe Drew says: "Wal, I'll be whupped."

"Be whupped," Joe said, "and whar you goen?"
"Oh, I'm just visiten back whar I done my growen
In the section between the rivers,
Fer I bin out West and taken my share
And I reckin my luck helt out fer fair,
So I done come home," Little Billie said,
"To see my folks if'n they ain't dead."
"Ain't dead," Joe answered, and shook his head,
"But that's the best a man kin say,

Fer hit looked lak when you went away
You taken West yore Pappy's luck
And maybe now you kin bring hit back
To the section between the rivers."
Little Billie laughed and jingled his pockets and said: "Ain't
    nuthen wrong with my luck."

And said: "Wal, I'll be gitten on home,
But after yore supper why don't you come
And we'll open a jug and you tell me the news
In the section between the rivers.
But not too early fer hit's my aim
To git some fun 'fore they know my name,
And tease 'em and fun 'em, fer you never guessed
I was Little Billie what went out West."
And Joe Drew said: "Durn if'n you always wuzn't a hand to git
    yore fun."

(Over the plain, over mountain and river, drawn,
Wanderer with slit-eyes adjusted to distance,

Drawn out of distance, drawn from the great plateau
Where the sky heeled in the unsagging wind and the cheek
    burned,
Who stood beneath the white peak that glimmered like a dream,
And spat, and it was morning and it was morning.
You lay among the wild plums and the kildees cried.
You lay in the thicket under the new leaves and the kildees
    cried,
For you all luck, for all the astuteness of your heart,
And would not stop and would not stop
And the clock ticked all night long in the furnished room
And would not stop
And the *El*-train passed on the quarters with a whish like a
    terrible broom

And would not stop
And there is always the sound of breathing in the next room
And it will not stop
And the waitress says, "Will that be all, sir, will that be all?"
And will not stop
And the valet says, "Will that be all, sir, will that be all?"
And will not stop
For nothing is ever all and nothing is ever all,
For all your experience and your expertness of human vices and
    of valor
At the hour when the ways are darkened.

Though your luck held and the market was always satisfactory,
Though the letter always came and your lovers were always true,
Though you always received the respect due to your position,
Though your hand never failed of its cunning and your glands
    always thoroughly knew their business,
Though your conscience was easy and you were assured of
    your innocence,
You became gradually aware that something was missing from
    the picture,
And upon closer inspection exclaimed: "Why, I'm not in it at
    all!"
Which was perfectly true.

Therefore you tried to remember when you had last had
        whatever it was you had lost,
But it was a long time back.
And you decided to retrace your steps from that point,
But it was a long way back.
It was nevertheless, absolutely essential to make the effort,
And since you had never been a man to be deterred by difficult
        circumstances,
You came back.
For there is no place like home.)

He joked them and he teased them and he had his fun
And they never guessed that he was the one
Had been Mammy's darling and Pappy's joy
When he was a great big whickering boy
In the land between the rivers,
And he jingled his pockets and he took his sop
And patted his belly which was full nigh to pop
And wiped the buttermilk out of his beard
And took his belch and up and reared
Back from the table and cocked his chair
And said: "Old man, ain't you got any fresh drinken water, this
        here ain't fresher'n a hoss puddle?"
And the old woman said: "Pappy, why don't you take the young
        gentleman down to the spring so he kin git hit good
        and fresh?"
And the old woman gave the old man a straight look.
She gave him the bucket but it was not empty but it was not
        water.

Oh, the stars are shining and the meadow is bright
But under the trees is dark and night
In the land between the rivers.
Oh, on the trace the fireflies spark
But under the trees is night and dark,
And way off yonder is the whippoorwill
And the owl off yonder hoots on the hill
But under the trees is dark and still
In the section between the rivers.

And the leaves hang down in the dark of the trees
And there is the spring in the dark of the trees
And there is the spring as black as ink
And one star in it caught through a chink
Of the leaves that hang down in the dark of the trees,
And the star is there but it does not wink.
And Little Billie gets down on his knees
And props his hands in the same old place
To sup the water at his ease;
And the star is gone but there is his face.
"Just help yoreself," Big Billie said;
Then set the hatchet in his head.
They went through his pockets and they buried him in the dark
     of the trees.
"I figgered he was a ripe 'un," the old man said.
"Yeah, but you wouldn't done nuthen hadn't bin fer me," the
     old woman said.
(The reflection is shadowy and the form not clear,
For the hour is late, is late, and scarcely a glimmer comes here
Under the leaf, the bough, in its innocence dark;
And under your straining face you can scarcely mark
The darkling gleam of your face little less than the water dark.

But perhaps what you lost was lost in the pool long ago
When childlike you lost it and then in your innocence rose to
     go
After kneeling, as now, with your thirst beneath the leaves:
And years it lies here and dreams in the depth and grieves,
More faithful than mother or father in the light or dark of the
     leaves.

But after, after the irrefutable modes and marches,
After waters that never quench the thirst in the throat that
     parches,
After the sleep that sieves the long day's dubieties
And the cricket's corrosive wisdom under the trees,
After the rumor of wind and the bright anonymities,
You come weary of greetings and the new friend's smile,
Weary in art of the stranger, worn with your wanderer's wile,

Weary of innocence and the husks of Time,
Prodigal, back to the homeland of no-Time,
To ask forgiveness and the patrimony of your crime;

And kneel in the untutored night as to demand
What gift—oh, father, father—from that dissevering hand?)

"And whar's Little Billie?" Joe Drew said.
"Air you crazy," said Big, "and plum outa yore head,
Fer you knows he went West nigh ten long year?"
"Went West," Joe said, "but I seen him here
In the section between the rivers,
Riden up the trace as big as you please
With a long black coat comen down to his knees
And a big black beard comen down to his guts
And silver mountens on his pistol-butts
And he said out West how he done struck
It rich and wuz bringen you back yore luck."
"I shore-God could use some luck," Big Billie said,
But his woman wet her lips and craned her head
And said: "Come riden with a big black beard, you say?"
And Joe: "Oh, hit wuz Billie as big as day."
And the old man's eyes bugged out of a sudden and he croaked
          like a sick bull-frog and said: "Come riden with a long
          black coat?"

Oh, the night is still and the grease-lamp low
And the old man's breath comes wheeze and slow.
Oh, the blue flame sucks on the old rag wick
And the old woman's breath comes sharp and quick,
And there isn't a sound under the roof
But her breath's hiss and his breath's puff,
And there isn't a sound outside the door
As they hearken but cannot hear any more
The creak of the saddle or the plop of the hoof,
For a long time now Joe Drew's been gone
And left them sitting there alone
While the dark outside gets big and still,
For the owl doesn't hoot off there on the hill

Any more and is quiet, and the whippoorwill
Is quiet in the dark of the trees and still
In the land between the rivers.
And so they sit and breathe and wait
And breathe while the night gets big and late,
And neither of them gives move or stir
And she won't look at him and he won't look at her.
He doesn't look at her but he says: "Git me the spade."

She grabbled with her hands and he dug with the spade
Where the leaves let down the dark and shade
In the land between the rivers.
She grabbled like a dog in the hole they made,
But stopped of a sudden and then she said,
"I kin put my hand on his face."
They light up a pine-knot and lean at the place
Where the man in the black coat slumbers and lies
With trash in his beard and dirt on his face;
And the torch-flame shines in his wide-open eyes.
Down the old man leans with the flickering flame
And moves his lips, says: "Tell me his name."
"Ain't Billie, ain't Billie," the old woman cries,
"Oh, hit ain't my Billie, fer he wuz little
And helt to my skirt while I stirred the kittle
And called me Mammy and hugged me tight
And come in the house when hit fell night."
But the old man leans down with the flickering flame
And croaks: "But tell me his name."
"Oh, he ain't got none, fer he just come riden
From some fer place whar he'd bin biden,
And ain't got a name and never had none,
But Billie, my Billie, he had one,
And hit wuz Billie, hit wuz his name."
But the old man croaked: "Tell me his name."
"Oh, he ain't got none and hit's all the same,
But Billie had one, and he wuz little
And offen his chin I would wipe the spittle
And wiped the drool and kissed him thar
And counted his toes and kissed him whar

The little black mark wuz under his tit,
Shaped lak a clover under his left tit,
With a shape fer luck and I'd kiss hit—"
And the old man blinks in the pine-knot flare
And his mouth comes open like a fish for air,
Then he says right low, "I had nigh fergot."
"Oh, I kissed him on his little luck-spot
And I kissed and he'd laff as lak as not—"
The old man said: "Git his shirt open."
The old woman opened the shirt and there was the birthmark
        under the left tit.
It was shaped for luck.

(The bee knows, and the eel's cold ganglia burn,
And the sad head lifting to the long return,
Through brumal deeps, in the great unsolsticed coil,
Carries its knowledge, navigator without star,
And under the stars, pure in its clamorous toil,
The goose hoots north where the starlit marshes are.
The salmon heaves at the fall, and, wanderer, you
Heave at the great fall of Time, and gorgeous, gleam
In the powerful arc, and anger and outrage like dew,
In your plunge, fling, and plunge to the thunderous stream:
Back to the silence, back to the pool, back
To the high pool, motionless, and the unmurmuring dream.
And you, wanderer, back,
Brother to pinion and the pious fin that cleave
Their innocence of air and the disinfectant flood
And wing and welter and weave
The long compulsion and the circuit hope
Back,
And bear through that limitless and devouring fluidity
The itch and humble promise which is home.
And you, wanderer, back,
For the beginning is death and the end may be life,
For the beginning was definition and the end may be definition,
And our innocence needs, perhaps, new definition,
And the wick needs the flame
But the flame needs the wick.

And the father waits for the son.
The hour is late,
The scene familiar even in shadow,
The transaction brief,
And you, wanderer, back,
After the striving and the wind's word,
To kneel
Here in the evening empty of wind or bird,
To kneel in the sacramental silence of evening
At the feet of the old man
Who is evil and ignorant and old,
To kneel
With the little black mark under your heart,
Which is your name,
Which is shaped for luck,
Which is your luck.)

BEARDED OAKS

The oaks, how subtle and marine,
Bearded, and all the layered light
Above them swims; and thus the scene,
Recessed, awaits the positive night.

So, waiting, we in the grass now lie
Beneath the languorous tread of light:
The grasses, kelp-like, satisfy
The nameless motions of the air.

Upon the floor of light, and time,
Unmurmuring, of polyp made,
We rest; we are, as light withdraws,
Twin atolls on a shelf of shade.

Ages to our construction went,
Dim architecture, hour by hour:
And violence, forgot now, lent
The present stillness all its power.

The storm of noon above us rolled,
Of light the fury, furious gold,
The long drag troubling us, the depth:
Dark is unrocking, unrippling, still.

Passion and slaughter, ruth, decay
Descend, minutely whispering down,
Silted down swaying streams, to lay
Foundation for our voicelessness.

All our debate is voiceless here,
As all our rage, the rage of stone;
If hope is hopeless, then fearless fear,
And history is thus undone.

Our feet once wrought the hollow street
With echo when the lamps were dead
At windows, once our headlight glare
Disturbed the doe that, leaping, fled.

I do not love you less that now
The caged heart makes iron stroke,
Or less that all that light once gave
The graduate dark should now revoke.

We live in time so little time
And we learn all so painfully,
That we may spare this hour's term
To practice for eternity.

TO A LITTLE GIRL, ONE YEAR OLD,
IN A RUINED FORTRESS

To Rosanna

I. SIROCCO

To a place of ruined stone we brought you, and sea-reaches.
Rocca: fortress, hawk-heel, lion-paw, clamped on a hill.
A hill, no. Sea cliff, and crag-cocked, the embrasures
    commanding the beaches,
Range easy, with most fastidious mathematic and skill.

Philipus me fecit: he of Spain, the black-browed, the anguished,
For whom nothing prospered, though he loved God.

His arms, great scutcheon of stone, once at drawbridge, have
    now languished
Long in the moat, under garbage; at moat-brink, rosemary with
    blue, thistle with gold bloom, nod.

Sun blaze and cloud tatter, it is the sirocco, the dust swirl is
    swirled
Over the bay face, mounts air like gold gauze whirled; it
    traverses the blaze-blue of water.
We have brought you where geometry of a military rigor
    survives its own ruined world,
And sun regilds your gilt hair, in the midst of your laughter.

Rosemary, thistle, clutch stone. Far hangs Giannutri in blue air.
    Far to that blueness the heart aches,
And on the exposed approaches the last gold of gorse bloom, in
    the sirocco, shakes.

II. GULL'S CRY

White goose by palm tree, palm ragged, among stones the
    white oleander,
And the she-goat, brown, under pink oleander, waits.
I do not think that anything in the world will move, not goat,
    not gander.

Goat droppings are fresh in the hot dust; not yet the beetle; the
    sun beats,
And under blue shadow of mountain, over blue-braiding sea-
    shadow,
The gull hangs white; whiter than white against mountain-
    mass,
The gull extends motionless on shelf of air, on substance of
    shadow.
The gull, at an eye-blink, will, into the astonishing statement of
    sun, pass.

All night, next door, the defective child cried; now squats in the
    dust where the lizard goes.
The wife of the *gobbo* sits under vine leaves, she suffers, her
    eyes glare.
The engaged ones sit in the privacy of bemusement, heads bent:
    the classic pose.
Let the beetle work, the gull comment the irrelevant anguish
    of air,

But at your laughter let the molecular dance of the stone-dark
    glimmer like joy in the stone's dream,
And in that moment of possibility, let *gobbo, gobbo's* wife,
    and us, and all, take hands and sing: redeem, redeem!

III. THE CHILD NEXT DOOR

The child next door is defective because the mother,
Seven brats already in that purlieu of dirt,
Took a pill, or did something to herself she thought would not
    hurt,
But it did, and no good, for there came this monstrous other.

The sister is twelve. Is beautiful like a saint.
Sits with the monster all day, with pure love, calm eyes.
Has taught it a trick, to make *ciao*, Italian-wise.
It crooks hand in that greeting. She smiles her smile without
    taint.

I come, and her triptych beauty and joy stir hate
—Is it hate?—in my heart. Fool, doesn't she know that the
    process
Is not that joyous or simple, to bless, or unbless,
The malfeasance of nature or the filth of fate?
Can it bind or loose, that beauty in that kind,
Beauty of benediction? I trust our hope to prevail

That heart-joy in beauty be wisdom, before beauty fail
And be gathered like air in the ruck of the world's wind!

I think of your goldness, of joy, how empires grind, stars are
    hurled.
I smile stiff, saying *ciao,* saying *ciao,* and think: this is the
    world.

IV. THE FLOWER

Above the beach, the vineyard
Terrace breaks to the seaward
Drop, where the cliffs fail
To a clutter of manganese shale.
Some is purple, some powdery-pale.
But the black lava-chunks stand off
The sea's grind, or indolent chuff.
The lava will withstand
The sea's beat, or insinuant hand,
And protect our patch of sand.

It is late. The path from the beach
Crawls up. I take you. We reach
The vineyard, and at that path angle
The hedge obtrudes a tangle

Of leaf and green bulge and a wrangle
Bee-drowsy and blowsy with white bloom,
Scarcely giving the passer-by room.
We know that that blossomy mass
Will brush our heads as we pass,
And at knee there's gold gorse and blue clover,
And at ankle, blue *malva* all over
—Plus plants I don't recognize
With my non-botanical eyes.
We approach, but before we get there,
If no breeze stirs that green lair,
The scent and sun-honey of air
Is too sweet comfortably to bear.
I carry you up the hill.
In my arms you are sweet and still.
We approach your special place,
And I am watching your face
To see the sweet puzzlement grow,
And then recognition glow.
Recognition explodes in delight.
You leap like spray, or like light.
Despite my arm's tightness,
You leap in gold-glitter and brightness.
You leap like a fish-flash in bright air,
And reach out. Yes, I'm well aware
That this is the spot, and hour,
For you to demand your flower.

When first we came this way
Up from the beach, that day
That seems now so long ago,
We moved bemused and slow
In the season's pulse and flow.
Bemused with sea, and slow
With June heat and perfume,
We paused here, and plucked you a bloom.
So here you always demand
Your flower to hold in your hand,
And the flower must be white,

For you have your own ways to compel
Observance of this ritual.
You hold it and sing with delight.
And your mother, for our own delight,
Picks one of the blue flowers there,
To put in your yellow hair.
That done, we go on our way
Up the hill, toward the end of the day.

But the season has thinned out.
From the bay edge below, the shout
Of a late bather reaches our ear,
Coming to the vineyard here
By more than distance thinned.
The bay is in shadow, the wind
Nags the shore to white.
The mountain prepares the night.
By the vineyard we have found
No bloom worthily white,
And the few we have found
Not disintegrated to the ground
Are by season and sea-salt browned.
We give the best one to you.
It is ruined, but will have to do.
Somewhat better the blue blossoms fare.
We find one for your hair,
And you sing as though human need
Were not for perfection. We proceed
Past floss-borne or sloughed-off seed,
Past curled leaf and dry pod,
And the blue blossom will nod
With your head's drowsy gold nod.

Let all seasons pace their power,
As this has paced to this hour.
Let season and season devise
Their possibilities.
Let the future reassess
All past joy, and past distress,

Till we know Time's deep intent,
And the last integument
Of the past shall be rent
To show how all things bent
Their energies to that hour
When you first demanded your flower.
And in that image let
Both past and future forget,
In clasped communal ease,
Their brute identities.

The path lifts up ahead
To the *rocca*, supper, bed.
We move in the mountain's shade.
But the mountain is at our back.
Ahead, climbs the coast-cliff track.
The valley between is dim.
Ahead, on the cliff rim,
The *rocca* clasps its height.
It accepts the incipient night.
Just once we look back.
On sunset, a white gull is black.
It hangs over the mountain crest.
It hangs on that saffron west.
It makes its outcry.

It slides down the sky.
East now, it catches the light.
Its black has gone again white,
And over the *rocca's* height
It gleams in the last light.
It has sunk from our sight.
Beyond the cliff is night.

It sank on unruffled wing.
We hear the sea rustling.

It will rustle all night, darling.

V. Colder Fire

It rained toward day. The morning came sad and white
With silver of sea-sadness and defection of season.
Our joys and convictions are sure, but in that wan light
We moved—your mother and I—in muteness of spirit past
    logical reason.

Now sun, afternoon, and again summer-glitter on sea.
As you to a bright toy, the heart leaps. The heart unlocks
Joy, though we know, shamefaced, the heart's weather should
    not be
Merely a reflex to solstice, or sport of some aggrieved equinox.

No, the heart should be steadfast: I know that.
And I sit in the late-sunny lee of the watch-house,
At the fortress point, you on my knee now, and the late
White butterflies over gold thistle conduct their ritual carouse.
In whisperless carnival, in vehemence of gossamer,
Pale ghosts of pale passions of air, the white wings weave.
In tingle and tangle of arabesque, they mount light, pair by pair,
As though that tall light were eternal indeed, not merely the
    summer's reprieve.

You leap on my knee, you exclaim at the sun-stung gyration.
And the upper air stirs, as though the vast stillness of sky
Had stirred in its sunlit sleep and made a suspiration,
A luxurious languor of breath, as after love, there is a sigh.

But enough, for the highest sun-scintillant pair are gone
Seaward, past rampart and cliff borne, over blue sea-gleam.
Close to my chair, to a thistle, a butterfly sinks now, flight done.
By gold bloom of thistle, white wings pulse under the sky's
    dream.

The sky's dream is enormous, I lift up my eyes.
In sunlight a tatter of mist clings high on the mountain-mass.
The mountain is under the sky, and there the gray scarps rise
Past paths where on their appointed occasions men climb, and
    pass.

ROBERT PENN WARREN   137

Past grain-patch, last apron of vineyard, last terrace of olive,
Past chestnut, past cork grove, where the last carts can go,
Past camp of the charcoal maker, where coals glow in the black
     hive,
The scarps, gray, rise up. Above them is that place I know.

The pines are there, they are large, a deep recess,
Shelf above scarp, enclave of rock, a glade
Benched and withdrawn in the mountain-mass, under the
     peak's duress.
We came there—your mother and I—and rested in that severe
     shade.

Pine-blackness mist-tangled, the peak black above: the glade
     gives
On the empty threshold of air, the hawk-hung delight
Of distance unspooled and bright space spilled—ah, the heart
     thrives!
We stood in that shade and saw sea and land lift in the far
     light.

Now the butterflies dance, time-tattered and disarrayed.
I watch them. I think how above that far scarp's sunlit wall
Mist threads in silence the darkness of boughs, and in that
     shade
Condensed moisture gathers at needle-tip. It glitters, will fall.

I cannot interpret for you this collocation
Of memories. You will live your own life, and contrive
The language of your own heart, but let that conversation,
In the last analysis, be always of whatever truth you would live.

For fire flames but in the heart of a colder fire.
All voice is but echo caught from a soundless voice.
Height is not deprivation of valley, nor defect of desire,
But defines, for the fortunate, that joy in which all joys
     should rejoice.

SCHOOL LESSON BASED ON WORD OF
TRAGIC DEATH OF ENTIRE GILLUM FAMILY

They weren't so bright, or clean, or clever,
   And their noses were sometimes imperfectly blown,
But they always got to school the weather whatever,
   With old lard pail full of fried pie, smoked ham, and corn pone.

Tow hair was thick 's a corn-shuck mat.
   They had milky blue eyes in matching pairs,
And barefoot or brogan, when they sat,
   Their toes were the kind that hook round the legs of chairs.

They had adenoids to make you choke,
   And buttermilk breath, and their flannels asteam,
And sat right mannerly while teacher spoke,
   But when book-time came their eyes were glazed and adream.

There was Dollie-May, Susie-May, Forrest, Sam, Brother—
   Thirteen down to eight the stairsteps ran.
They had popped right natural from their big fat mother—
   The clabber kind that can catch just by honing after a man.

In town, Gillum stopped you, he'd say: "Say, mister,
   I'll name you what's true fer folks, ever-one.
Human-man ain't much more'n a big blood blister.
   All red and proud-swole, but one good squeeze and he's gone.

"Take me, ain't wuth lead and powder to perish,
   Just some spindle bone stuck in a pair of pants,
But a man's got his chaps to love and to cherish,
   And raise up and larn'em so they kin git they chance."

So mud to the hub, or dust to the hock,
   God his helper, wet or dry,
Old Gillum swore by God and by cock,
   He'd git'em larned before his own time came to die.

ROBERT PENN WARREN   139

That morning blew up cold and wet,
  All the red-clay road was curdled as curd,
And no Gillums there for the first time yet.
  The morning drones on. Stove spits. Recess. Then the word.

Dollie-May was combing Susie-May's head.
  Sam was feeding, Forrest milking, got nigh through.
Little Brother just sat on the edge of his bed.
  Somebody must have said: "Pappy, now what you aimin' to
    do?"

An ice pick is a subtle thing.
  The puncture's small, blood only a wisp.
It hurts no more than a bad bee sting.
  When the sheriff got there the school-bread was long burned
    to a crisp.

In the afternoon silence the chalk would scrape.
  We sat and watched the windowpanes steam,
Blur the old corn field and accustomed landscape.
  Voices came now faint in our intellectual dream.

Which shoe—yes, which—was Brother putting on?
  That was something, it seemed, you just had to know.
But nobody knew, all afternoon,
  Though we studied and studied, as hard as we could, to know,

Studying the arithmetic of losses,
  To be prepared when the next one,
By fire, flood, foe, cancer, thrombosis,
  Or Time's slow malediction, came to be undone.

We studied all afternoon, till getting on to sun.
There would be another lesson, but we were too young to take
  up that one.

VII. TELL ME A STORY

(*Part VII of Audubon*: A *Vision*)

[A]

Long ago, in Kentucky, I, a boy, stood
By a dirt road, in first dark, and heard
The great geese hoot northward.
I could not see them, there being no moon
And the stars sparse. I heard them.

I did not know what was happening in my heart.

It was the season before the elderberry blooms,
Therefore they were going north.

The sound was passing northward.

[B]

Tell me a story.

In this century, and moment, of mania,
Tell me a story.

Make it a story of great distances, and starlight.

The name of the story will be Time,
But you must not pronounce its name.

Tell me a story of deep delight.

ROBERT PENN WARREN   141

HEART OF AUTUMN

Wind finds the northwest gap, fall comes.
Today, under gray cloud-scud and over gray
Wind-flicker of forest, in perfect formation, wild geese
Head for a land of warm water, the *boom*, the lead pellet.

Some crumple in air, fall. Some stagger, recover control,
Then take the last glide for a far glint of water. None
Knows what has happened. Now, today, watching
How tirelessly V upon V arrows the season's logic,

Do I know my own story? At least, they know
When the hour comes for the great wing-beat. Sky-strider,
Star-strider—they rise, and the imperial utterance,
Which cries out for distance, quivers in the wheeling sky.

That much they know, and in their nature know
The path of pathlessness, with all the joy
Of destiny fulfulling its own name.
I have known time and distance, but not why I am here.

Path of logic, path of folly, all
The same—and I stand, my face lifted now skyward,
Hearing the high beat, my arms outstretched in the tingling
Process of transformation, and soon tough legs,

With folded feet, trail in the sounding vacuum of passage,
And my heart is impacted with a fierce impulse
To unwordable utterance—
Toward sunset, at a great height.

A Selected Bibliography

I. PRIMARY SOURCES

A. Books

Crane, Hart. *The Complete Poems and Selected Letters and Prose of Hart Crane.* Edited by Brom Weber. New York: Liveright, 1986.

Davidson, Donald. *An Outland Piper.* Boston: Houghton Mifflin, 1924.

_____. *The Tall Men.* Boston: Houghton Mifflin, 1927.

_____. *Lee in the Mountains and Other Poems.* Boston: Houghton Mifflin 1938 (reissued New York: Scribner's, 1949).

_____. *The Long Street.* Nashville: Vanderbilt University Press, 1961.

_____. *Poems 1922–61.* Nashville: Vanderbilt University Press, 1966.

_____. *Singin' Billy: A Folk Opera.* Glendale, S.C.: Southron Press, 1985.

Fletcher, John Gould. *Selected Poems.* Edited by Lucas Carpenter and Leighton Rudolph. Fayetteville: University of Arkansas Press, 1988.

_____. *Fugitives: An Anthology of Verse.* New York: Harcourt, Brace, 1928.

Graves, Robert. *New Collected Poems.* New York: Doubleday, 1977.

Moore, Merrill. *The Noise That Time Makes.* New York: Harcourt, Brace, 1929.

_____. *Six Sides to a Man.* New York: Harcourt, Brace, 1935.

_____. *Poems from The Fugitive*. New York: Beekman Hill Press, 1936.

_____. *Sonnets from The Fugitive*. Boston: Caduceus Press, 1937.

_____. *15 Poems from The Fugitive*. Boston: Caduceus Press, 1938.

_____. *M: One Thousand Autobiographical Sonnets*. New York: Harcourt, Brace, 1938.

_____. *Sonnets from New Directions* (with a preface by William Carlos Williams). Norfolk, Conn: New Directions, 1938.

_____. *Notes and Poems* (private publication), 1940.

_____. *Case Record from a Sonnetorium*. New York: Twayne, 1951.

_____. *More Clinical Sonnets*. New York: Twayne, 1953.

_____. *Poems of American Life* (with an introduction by Louis Untermeyer). New York: Philosophical Library, 1958.

_____. *The Dance of Death*. Brooklyn: I.E. Rubin, 1959.

Ransom, John Crowe. *Poems About God*. New York: Henry Holt, 1919.

_____. *Chills and Fever*. New York: Alfred Knopf, 1924.

_____. *Two Gentlemen in Bonds*. New York: Alfred Knopf, 1927.

_____. *Selected Poems*. New York: Alfred Knopf, 1945.

_____. *Selected Poems* (revised and enlarged edition). New York: Alfred Knopf, 1963.

_____. *Selected Poems* (third edition, revised and enlarged). New York: Alfred Knopf, 1974.

Riding (Gottschalk Jackson), Laura. *The Poems of Laura Riding* (A New Edition of the 1938 Collection). Manchester, England: Carcanet New Press, 1980.

_____. *Selected Poems in Five Sets*. New York: Norton, 1970.

Tate, Allen. *Mr. Pope and Other Poems*. New York: Minton, Balch, 1928.

_____. *Poems: 1928–1931*. New York: Scribner's, 1932.

_____. *The Mediterranean and Other Poems*. New York: Alcestis Press, 1936.

_____. *Selected Poems*. New York: Scribner's, 1937.

_____. *The Winter Sea*. Cummington, Mass.: Cummington Press, 1944.

_____. *Poems: 1922–1947*. New York: Scribner's, 1948 (reissued, with additions, 1960.) (Paperback edition, Denver: Alan Swallow, 1961).

_____. *The Swimmers and Other Selected Poems*. New York: Scribner's, 1970.

_____. *Collected Poems, 1919–1976*. New York: Farrar Straus Giroux, 1977.

_____ and Ridley Wills.

_____. *The Golden Mean and Other Poems* (a parody of *The Fugitive*). Nashville, 1923.

Warren, Robert Penn. *Thirty-six Poems*. New York: Alcestis Press, 1935.

_____. *Eleven Poems on the Same Theme*. Norfolk, Conn: New Directions, 1942.

_____. *Selected Poems, 1923–1943*. New York: Harcourt, Brace, 1944.

_____. *Promises: Poems 1954–1956*. New York: Random House, 1957.

_____. *You, Emperors, and Others: Poems 1957–1960*. New York: Random House, 1960.

_____. *Selected Poems, 1923–1966*. New York: Random House, 1966.

_____. *Incarnations: Poems 1966–68*. New York: Random House, 1968.

_____. *Audubon: A Vision*. New York: Random House, 1969.

_____. *Or Else: Poem/Poems 1968–1974*. New York: Random House, 1974.

_____. *Now and Then: Poems 1976–1978*. New York: Random House, 1978.

_____. *Being Here: Poetry 1977–1980*. New York: Random House, 1980.

_____. *Rumor Verified: Poems 1979–1980*. New York: Random House, 1981.

_____. *Chief Joseph of the Nez Perce*. New York: Random House, 1983.

_____. *New and Selected Poems, 1923–1985*. New York: Random House, 1985.

Wills, Jesse. *Poems Early and Late*. Nashville: Vanderbilt University Press, 1959.

_____. *Conversation Piece and Other Poems*. Nashville, 1965.

_____. *Nashville and Other Poems*. Nashville: Fantasie Press, 1973.

_____. *Selected Poems*. Nashville: Vanderbilt University Press, 1975.

B. Magazines

The Fugitive. Nashville, April, 1922–December, 1925. Four Volumes, Nineteen Numbers.

The Fugitive: April, 1922 to December, 1925. Reprinted in One Volume, with an Introduction by Donald Davidson. Gloucester, Mass.: Peter Smith, 1967.

II. SECONDARY SOURCES

A. Books

Bedient, Calvin. *In the Heart's Last Kingdom: Robert Penn Warren's Major Poetry*. Cambridge: Harvard University Press, 1984.

_____. *A Bibliographical Guide to the Study of Southern Literature*. Edited by Louis D. Rubin, Jr. Baton Rouge: Louisiana State University Press, 1969.

Bloom, Harold. *Robert Penn Warren*. New York: Chelsea, 1986.

Bohner, Charles H. *Robert Penn Warren*. New York: Twayne, 1981.

Bradbury, John M. *The Fugitives: A Critical Account*. Chapel Hill: University of North Carolina Press, 1958.

_____. *Renaissance in the South: A Critical History of the Literature, 1920–1960*. Chapel Hill: University of North Carolina Press, 1963.

Clark, William Bedford. *Critical Essays on Robert Penn Warren*. New York: Hall, 1981.

Conkin, Paul Keith. *Gone with the Ivy: A Biography of Vanderbilt University*. Knoxville: University of Tennessee Press, 1985.

_____. *The Southern Agrarians*. Knoxville: University of Tennessee Press, 1988.

Cowan, Louise. *The Fugitive Group: A Literary History*. Baton Rouge: Louisiana State University Press, 1959.

Davidson, Donald. *The Attack on Leviathan*. Chapel Hill: University of North Carolina Press, 1938.

_____. *The Tennessee*. (Two volumes). New York: Rinehart, 1946–48, volume 1 new edition, Nashville: J.S. Sanders & Company, 1991.

_____. *Still Rebels, Still Yankees and Other Essays*. Baton Rouge: Louisiana State University Press, 1957.

_____. *Southern Writers in the Modern World*. Athens: University of Georgia Press, 1958.

_____. *The Spyglass: Views and Reviews, 1924–1930*. Nashville: Vanderbilt University Press, 1963.

_____. *The Literary Correspondence of Donald Davidson and Allen Tate*. Edited by John Tyree Fain and Thomas Daniel Young. Athens: University of Georgia Press, 1974.

Edgar, Walter B., editor. *A Southern Renaissance Man: Views of Robert Penn Warren*. Baton Rouge: Louisiana State University Press, 1984.

_____. *Encyclopedia of Southern Culture*. Edited by Charles Reagan

Wilson and William Ferris. Chapel Hill: University of North Carolina Press, 1989.

_____. *Fifty Southern Writers After 1900: A Bio-Bibliographical Sourcebook*. Edited by Joseph M. Flora and Robert Bain. New York: Greenwood Press, 1987.

Fletcher, John Gould. *Selected Essays*. Edited by Lucas Carpenter. Fayetteville: University of Arkansas Press, 1989.

_____. *Fugitives' Reunion: Conversations at Vanderbilt, May 3–5, 1956*. Edited by R.R. Purdy. Nashville: Vanderbilt University Press, 1959.

Graves, Richard Perceval. *Robert Graves: The Years With Laura, 1926–1940*. New York: Viking Penguin, 1990.

Graves, Robert and Laura Riding. *A Survey of Modernist Poetry*. New York: Haskell Press, 1969 (reprint of 1928 book).

Gray, Richard. *Robert Penn Warren: A Collection of Critical Essays*. Englewood Cliffs, New Jersey: Prentice Hall, 1980.

_____. *History of Southern Literature*. Edited by Louis Rubin, et al. Baton Rouge: Louisiana State University Press, 1985.

Havard, William C. and Walter Sullivan, editors. *Band of Prophets: The Vanderbilt Agrarians After Fifty Years* Baton Rouge: Louisiana State University Press, 1982.

_____. *Homage to Robert Penn Warren: A Collection of Critical Essays*. Edited by Frank Graziano and Hilton Kramer. New York: Logbridge-Rhodes, 1981.

_____. *I'll Take My Stand: The South and the Agrarian Tradition*. By Twelve Southerners. New York: Harper, 1930. (Reissued as a Harper Torchbook, 1962).

Johnson, Stanley. *Professor*. New York: Harcourt, Brace, 1925.

Justus, James H. *The Achievement of Robert Penn Warren*. Baton Rouge: Louisiana State University Press, 1981.

Meiners, R.K. *The Last Alternatives: A Study of the Works of Allen Tate*. Denver: Alan Swallow, 1963.

Merrill Moore. *The Fugitive: Clippings and Comment*. Boston, 1939.

Nakadate, Neil. *Robert Penn Warren: Critical Essays*. Lexington: The University Press of Kentucky, 1981.

O'Brien, Michael. *The Idea of the South, 1920–1941* Baltimore: Johns Hopkins Press, 1979.

Poenicke, Klaus. *Robert Penn Warren: Kunstwerk und Kritische Theorie*. Heidelberg: Carl Winter Universitätsverlag, 1959.

Quinlan, Kieran. *John Crowe Ransom's Secular Faith*. Baton Rouge: Louisiana State University Press, 1989.

Ransom, John Crowe. *God Without Thunder*. New York: Harcourt, Brace, 1930.

_____. *The World's Body*. New York: Scribner's, 1938.

_____. *The New Criticism*. Norfolk, Conn.: New Directions, 1941.

_____. *Beating the Bushes: Selected Essays 1941–1970*. New York: New Directions, 1972.

_____. *Selected Letters of John Crowe Ransom*. Edited by Thomas Daniel Young and George Core. Baton Rouge: Louisiana State University Press, 1985.

_____. *John Crowe Ransom: A Tribute from the Community of Letters*. Edited by D. David Long and Michael R. Burr. Gambier, Ohio, 1964.

_____. *Selected Essays*. Edited by Thomas Daniel Young and John Hindle. Baton Rouge: Louisiana State University Press, 1984.

Rubin, Louis. *The Faraway Country: Writers of the Modern South*. Seattle: University of Washington Press, 1963.

_____. *The Wary Fugitives: Four Poets and the South*. Baton Rouge: Louisiana State University Press, 1978.

_____. *The American South: Portrait of a Culture*. Baton Rouge: Louisiana State University Press, 1980.

_____ and Robert Jacobs. *South: Modern Southern Literature in its Cultural Setting*. New York: Doubleday Dolphin, 1961.

_____. *Southern Renascence: The Literature of the Modern South*. Baltimore: Johns Hopkins Press, 1953.

Runyon, Randolph Paul. *The Braided Dream: Robert Penn Warren's Later Poetry*. Lexington: University Press of Kentucky, 1990.

Squires, Radcliffe. *Allen Tate: A Literary Biography*. New York: Pegasus, 1971. (Editor)

_____. *Allen Tate and His Work: Critical Evaluations*. Minneapolis: University of Minnesota Press, 1971.

Schöpp, Josef. *Allen Tate: Tradition als Bauprinzip dualistischen Dichtens*. Bonn: Bouvier Verlag Herbert Grundmann, 1975.

_____. *Southern Writers: A Biographical Dictionary*. Edited by Joseph M. Flora and Louis D. Rubin, Jr. Baton Rouge: Louisiana State University Press, 1979.

Stewart, John L. *John Crowe Ransom*. Minneapolis: University of Minnesota Press, 1962.

Tate, Allen. *Stonewall Jackson*. New York: Minton, Balch, 1928. New edition, Nashville: J.S. Sanders & Company, 1991.

_____. *Jefferson Davis*. New York: Minton, Balch, 1929.

_____. *Reactionary Essays on Poetry and Ideas*. New York: Scribner's, 1936.

_____. *Who Owns America? A New Declaration of Independence.* Freeport, NY: Books for Library Press, 1970 (reprint of 1936)

_____. *The Fathers.* New York: Putnam, 1938. (Reissued by Denver: Alan Swallow, 1960).

_____. *Reason in Madness.* New York: Putnam, 1941.

_____. *On the Limits of Poetry.* New York: Swallow, 1948.

_____. *The Forlorn Demon.* Chicago: Henry Regnery, 1953.

_____. *Sixty American Poets.* Selected with preface and critical notes by Allen Tate. Washington: Library of Congress, 1954.

_____. *The Man of Letters in the Modern World.* New York: Meridian Books, 1955.

_____. *Collected Essays.* Denver: Alan Swallow, 1959.

_____. *The Hovering Fly and Other Essays.* Freeport, NY: Books for Library Press, 1968.

_____. *Essays of Four Decades.* Chicago: Swallow Press, 1968.

_____. *Memoirs and Opinions 1926–1974.* Chicago: Swallow Press, 1975.

_____. *The Republic of Letters in America: The Correspondence of John Peale Bishop and Allen Tate.* Edited by Thomas Daniel Young and John J. Hindle. Lexington: The University Press of Kentucky, 1981.

_____. *The Poetry Reviews of Allen Tate, 1924–1944.* Edited by Ashley Brown and Frances Neel Cheney. Baton Rouge: Louisiana State University Press, 1983.

_____. *The Lytle-Tate Letters: The Correspondence of Andrew Lytle and Allen Tate.* Edited by Thomas Daniel Young and Elizabeth Sarcone. Jackson: University Press of Mississippi, 1987.

Warren, Robert Penn. *John Brown: The Making of a Martyr.* New York: Payson & Clarke, 1929.

_____. *Night Rider.* Boston: Houghton Mifflin, 1939.

_____. *At Heaven's Gate.* New York: Harcourt, Brace, 1943.

_____. *All the King's Men.* New York: Harcourt, Brace, 1946.

_____. *The Circus in the Attic and Other Stories.* New York: Harcourt, Brace, 1947.

_____. *World Enough and Time.* New York: Random House, 1950.

_____. *Brother to Dragons.* New York: Random House, 1953.

_____. *Band of Angels.* New York: Random House, 1955.

_____. *Segregation.* New York: Random House, 1956.

_____. *Selected Essays.* New York: Random House, 1958.

_____. *The Cave.* New York: Random House, 1959.

_____. *Wilderness.* New York: Random House, 1961.

_____. *Flood*. New York: Random House, 1964.

_____. *Who Speaks for the Negro?* New York: Random House, 1965.

_____. *Meet Me in the Green Glen*. New York: Random House, 1971.

_____. *The Legacy of the Civil War*. Cambridge: Harvard University Press, 1983 (reprint of 1961 book).

_____. *Democracy and Poetry*. Cambridge: Harvard University Press, 1975.

_____. *A Place To Come To*. New York: Random House, 1977.

_____. *Robert Penn Warren Talking: Interviews 1950–1978*. Edited by Floyd C. Watkins and John T. Hiers. New York: Random House, 1980.

_____. *Jefferson Davis Gets His Citizenship Back*. Lexington: University Press of Kentucky, 1980.

_____. *A Robert Penn Warren Reader*. New York: Random House, 1987.

_____. *Portrait of a Father*. Lexington: University Press of Kentucky, 1988.

_____. *New and Selected Essays*. New York: Random House, 1989.

Watkins, Floyd C. *Then and Now: The Personal Past in the Poetry of Robert Penn Warren*. Lexington: University Press of Kentucky, 1982.

Winchell, Mark Royden (editor). *The Vanderbilt Tradition: Essays in Honor of Thomas Daniel Young*. Baton Rouge: Louisiana State University Press, 1991.

Young, Thomas Daniel. *Gentleman in a Dustcoat: A Biography of John Crowe Ransom*. Baton Rouge: Louisiana State University Press, 1976.

_____. *Selected Essays: 1965–1985*. Baton Rouge: Louisiana State University Press, 1990.

_____. *Tennessee Writers*. Knoxville: University of Tennessee Press, 1981.

_____ and M. Thomas Inge. *Donald Davidson: An Essay and a Bibliography*. Nashville: Vanderbilt University Press, 1965.

B. Essays and Articles

Blackmur, R.P. "*Anni Mirabiles 1921–25*: Reason in the Madness of Letters,"

_____. *Four Lectures Presented Under the Auspices of the Gertrude Clarke Whittall Poetry and Literature Fund* (Washington: Library of Congress, 1956).

Brooks, Cleanth. "T.S. Eliot and the American South," *Southern Review* (Autumn, 1985), 914–923.

———. "Faulkner and the Fugitive-Agrarians," in Dawson Fowler and Ann Abadie, editors, *The Southern Renaissance: Faulkner and Yoknapatawpha 1981*. Jackson: University Press of Mississippi, 1981.

———. "John Crowe Ransom As I Remember Him," The American Scholar (Spring, 1989), 211–233.

———. "Robert Penn Warren and American Idealism," *Sewanee Review* (Fall, 1989), 386–391.

———. "Episodes and Anecdotes in the Poetry of Robert Penn Warren," *Yale Review* (Summer, 1981), 551–567.

Cook, Martha E. "A Literary Friendship: Allen Tate and Donald Davidson," *Southern Review* (Fall, 1982), 739–754.

Core, George. "Mr. Tate and the Limits of Poetry," *Virginia Quarterly Review* (Winter, 1986), 105–114.

Cowan, Louise. "Innocent Doves: Ransom's Feminine Myth of the South," in J. Gerald Kennedy and David Mark Fogel, editors, *American Letters and the Historical Consciousness: Essays in Honor of Lewis P. Simpson*, Baton Rouge: Louisiana State University Press, 1987, 191–215.

Davidson, Donald. "The Thankless Muse and Her Fugitive Poets," *Southern Writers in the Modern World*. Athens: University of Georgia Press, 1958, 1–30.

Eliot, T.S. "Tradition and the Individual Talent," *Selected Essays* (New York: Harcourt, Brace, 1950), 3–11.

Fletcher, John Gould. "Two Elements in Poetry," *Saturday Review of Literature*, IV (Aug. 27, 1927), 65–66.

Gray, Richard. "In Search of a Past: The Fugitive Movement and the Major Traditionalists," Chapter 3 of *American Poetry of the Twentieth Century* (New York & London: Longmans, 1990), 101–156.

Hoffman, F.J., Chas. Allen, and Carolyn F. Ulrich. Chapter on *The Fugitive* in *The Little Magazine: A History and Bibliography*. Princeton: Princeton University Press, 1947, 116–124.

———. "Homage to John Crowe Ransom," *Sewanee Review*, LVI (July–Sept., 1948).

——— "Homage to John Crowe Ransom," *Shenandoah*, XIV (Spring, 1963).

——— "Special John Crowe Ransom Issue," *Mississippi Quarterly*, XXX (Winter, 1976–77).

_____. "Homage to Allen Tate," *Sewanee Review*, LXVII (Autumn, 1959).

_____. "In Honor of Allen Tate," *Poetry*, CXXXV (November, 1979).

_____. "The Legacy of Robert Penn Warren," *South Carolina Review*, 23 (Fall, 1990), 5–86.

Jarrell, Randall. "John Ransom's Poetry," *Poetry and the Age*. New York: Alfred Knopf, 1953, 96–111.

Meiners, R.K. "The End of History: Allen Tate's *Seasons of the Soul*," *Sewanee Review*, LXX (Winter, 1962), 34–80.

"On Returning," Interview with John Crowe Ransom, *Vanderbilt Alumnus*, XLVII (March–April 1962), 15–16, 45.

Pratt, William. "Fugitive from the South: Ransom at Kenyon," *The Old Northwest*, I (June, 1976), 181–196.

Ransom, John Crowe. "New Poets and Old Muses," *American Poetry at Mid-Century*. Washington: Library of Congress, 1958.

_____. "The Most Southern Poet," *Sewanee Review*, LXX (Spring, 1962), 202–207.

Rosenthal, M.L. "Robert Penn Warren's Poetry," *South Atlantic Quarterly*, LXII (1963), 499–507.

_____. "Laura Riding's Poetry: A Nice Problem," *Southern Review*, Winter, 1985, 89–95.

Smith, Dave. "He Prayeth Best Who Loveth Best: On Robert Penn Warren's Poetry," *The American Poetry Review* (Jan.–Feb., 1979), 4–8.

Southard, W.P. "The Religious Poetry of R.P. Warren," *Kenyon Review*, VII (Autumn, 1945), 653–676.

_____. "The Southern Literary Renaissance: A Symposium," *Shenandoah*, VI (Summer, 1955).

Spears, Monroe K. "Fugitive Group," in *The Concise Encyclopedia of English and American Poets and Poetry*, edited by Stephen Spender and Donald Hall. New York: Hawthorn Books, 1963. 141–142.

Squires, Radcliffe. "Mr. Tate: Whose Wreath Should Be a Moral," in *Aspects of American Poetry*, edited by Richard M. Ludwig. Columbus: Ohio State University Press, 1962.

Tate, Allen. "American Poetry Since 1920," *The Bookman*, LXVIII Jan., 1929), 504.

_____. "*The Fugitive* 1922–1925: A Personal Recollection Twenty Years After," *Princeton University Library Chronicle*, III (April, 1942), 75–84.

_____. "The Gaze Past, The Glance Present," *Sewanee Review*, LXX (Autumn, 1962), 671–673.

Van Doren, Mark. "First Glance," *Nation*, CXXVI (March 14, 1928), 295.

Warren, Robert Penn. "A Note on Three Southern Poets," in the Southern Number of *Poetry*, edited by Allen Tate. XL (May, 1932), 111–113.

_____. "John Crowe Ransom: A Study in Irony," *Virginia Quarterly Review*, XI (Jan., 1935), 93–112.

Watkins, Floyd C. " 'The body of this death' in Robert Penn Warren's Later Poems," *Kenyon Review* (Fall, 1988), 31–41.

Acknowledgments

Grateful acknowledgment is made to the following for permission to quote from copyright material:

JOHN CROWE RANSOM: All poems reprinted here are from *Selected Poems*, Third Edition, Revised and Enlarged, by John Crowe Ransom. Copyright 1924, 1927, 1934 by Alfred A. Knopf, Inc., and renewed 1952, 1955, 1962 by John Crowe Ransom. Reprinted by permission of Alfred A. Knopf, Inc.

STANLEY JOHNSON: "An Intellectual's Funeral" reprinted from *The Fugitive* magazine, April, 1922, I, 1. "A Sonnet of the Yellow Leaf" and "To a Park Swan" reprinted from *Fugitives: An Anthology of Verse*, New York: Harcourt, Brace & Co., 1928.

DONALD DAVIDSON: "Hermitage" and "Lines Written for Allen Tate on His Sixtieth Anniversary" reprinted from *The Long Street* by Donald Davidson, 1961, by permission of the Vanderbilt University Press. Other poems reprinted by permission of Mrs. Eric D. Bell.

ALEC BROCK STEVENSON: "He Who Loved Beauty" published in *Fugitives: An Anthology of Verse*, New York: Harcourt, Brace & Co., 1928. "Icarus in November" published in *A Vanderbilt Miscellany*, edited by Richmond Croom Beatty, Nashville: Vanderbilt University Press, 1944. "Sonnet on Death" published in the first edition of this anthology, New York: E. P. Dutton & Co, 1965, and "Death My Companion" and "A Hemlock at Sunset" printed here for the first time. All by permission of the author's son, Alec Brock Stevenson, Jr.

SIDNEY MTTRON HIRSCH: "Quodlibet" reprinted from *The Fugitive* magazine, April/May 1923, II, 6.

ALLEN TATE: "To Intellectual Detachment" reprinted from *The Fugitive* magazine, April, 1922, I, 1, and "Non Omnis Moriar" reprinted from *The Fugitive* magazine, October, 1922, I, 3; both by permission of Helen H. Tate. "Death of Little Boys," "The Mediterranean," "Aeneas at Washington," "Ode to the Confederate Dead," "Mr. Pope," "Last Days of Alice," "Seasons of the Soul," and "The Swimmers" from COLLECTED POEMS, 1919–1976 by Allen Tate. Copyright © 1977 by Allen Tate. Reprinted by permission of Farrar, Straus and Giroux, Inc.

MERRILL MOORE: "Cumae" reprinted from *The Fugitive* magazine, February, 1924, III, 1. "The Noise That Time Makes" and "The Book of How" reprinted from *Fugitives: An Anthology of Verse*, New York: Harcourt, Brace and Company, 1928. "Literature, The God, Its Ritual" reprinted from *Six Sides to a Man* by Merrill Moore, New York: Harcourt, Brace and Company, 1936. All four poems reprinted by permission of Ann Leslie Moore.

JESSE WILLS: "To a Tired Clerk" and "The Watchers" reprinted from *Early and Late* by Jesse Wills, 1959, by permission of the Vanderbilt University Press. "Half Said" and "The Fugitives" reprinted from *Selected Poems* by Jesse Wills, 1975, by permission of the Vanderbilt University Press.

LAURA RIDING: "Dimensions" reprinted from *The Fugitive* magazine, April/May, 1923, II, 8; "Starved" from *The Fugitive*, February, 1924, III, 1; "Summary for Alastor" from *The Fugitive* magazine, March 1925, IV, 1; "The Virgin of the Hills" and "The Only Daughter" from *The Fugitive* magazine, September, 1925, IV, 3. "The Poet's Corner" first appeared in *The Close Chaplet*, Adelphi, 1926, and is reprinted from *Fugitives: An Anthology of Verse*, New York: Harcourt, Brace & Co., 1928. All reprinted by permission of the author.

ROBERT GRAVES: "A Valentine" reprinted from *The Fugitive* magazine, December 1922, I, 4.

JOHN GOULD FLETCHER: "The Last Frontier" reprinted from *The Fugitive* magazine, February/March 1923, II, 5.

HART CRANE: "Stark Major" first appeared in *The Fugitive* magazine, August/September 1923, II, 8. It is reprinted from *The*

156   ACKNOWLEDGMENTS

WILLIAM PRATT was born in Shawnee, Oklahoma, in 1927, and educated in public schools and at the University of Oklahoma, where he earned a Bachelor's degree in English in 1949. At Vanderbilt University for graduate study, he received an M.A. in English in 1951, with a thesis on William Faulkner, and a Ph.D. in 1957, with a dissertation on Henry James, Ezra Pound, and T.S. Eliot. His graduate study included a year (1951–52) as a Rotary Foundation Fellow at the University of Glasgow, Scotland. In 1957, he joined the Department of English at Miami University in Oxford, Ohio, where he has been Professor of English since 1968, serving as Director of Freshman English, conducting a weekly series on educational television, lecturing on Modern Poetry and American Literature, and publishing essays, reviews, and translations in books and periodicals. Besides the first edition of *The Fugitive Poets* in 1965, he edited *The Imagist Poem: Modern Poetry in Miniature* in 1963, and with his wife, Anne Rich Pratt, translated René Taupin's *The Influence of French Symbolism on Modern American Poetry* in 1985, adding to it introductory and concluding essays, and co-edited with Robert Richardson a collection of essays, poems, maps and photographs issued in 1991 as a joint British-American *Homage to Imagism*. In 1975–76, he was Fulbright-Hays Professor of American Literature at University College, Dublin, Ireland, and in the fall of 1976, Resident Scholar at the Miami University European Center in Luxembourg. He has lectured widely on Modern Poetry in the United States and Europe, including the Yeats International Summer School in Ireland, the Ezra Pound International Conferences in England and Italy, and conferences of the International Society for Contemporary Literature and Theatre in France, Italy, Germany, England, Hungary, Yugoslavia, Greece, Spain, and Denmark.